What people are s~~~~~

Jami Lin, a licensed interior designer, has ~ elements of Feng Shui into her design busines~ her knowledge and experience available to ᴜᴇ masses in this power-packed, and highly informative book that includes spiritual principles, natural laws, sacred geometry, and astrology in an easy-to-use format.

NAPRA Review

I had recently become familiar with the principles of Feng Shui and was curious as to how I could implement said design in our living quarters. Late in 1994, on a recommendation, I had phoned Jami to arrange a consultation regarding my desire to update the decor of my tower suite condominium. However, with Jami finishing up the last details of her book, and with the impending holidays, we jointly decided to postpone our meeting until after the start of the new year.

Well, as often happens in life, I had released my obsession with creating space and moving Chi and was now obsessing on a more familiar agenda: the quest of my husband and I to conceive a child. As anyone familiar with protocol knows, the demanding schedule of an invitro-fertilization can be tedious, stress-filled, and immensely time consuming. We did however, join an internationally acclaimed astrologer for a seminar on meditation and the power of Jungian group thought.

During the workshop, she led us on an imaginary journey to Japan. After instructing us all in the ways of meditation and journeying, we were left to our own devices. As I was a touch skeptical, regarding the validity of such an exercise, imagine my surprise when I imagined myself right into a luxuriously appointed sacred temple, being escorted by two wizened monks to the temple elder who informed me that I may ask him one question.

My preoccupation with my faulty fertility precluded any other agenda, yet; as I struggled to mine the perfect words, this incredibly encouraging and strictly specific communique came from this beautiful being. He said, "Do not fret so. The child is near and will be home soon. You must be more patient, as this will surely be. You must prepare the child's space, and there is one who will be helpful here."

Now, suspending disbelief, let me reiterate, that I had buried my notions of redecorating, so imagine my shock as he then informed me, "You must contact Jami Lin. She is the facilitator to help create this environment. Even if she does nothing else in your home, she must help prepare for this child." And, poof, he was gone, and I was shown the way out and back to the point where the journey had originated.

I'm sure by now, you've guessed the rest. Jami Lin, designer, decorator extraordinaire, came, saw and conquered. Her talent combined with her extremely honed intuitive ability led me to make some decorative changes that I would have never imagined. Even taken back at some of her suggestions, I remembered my mystical moments and believed in her magic. Since the day Jami whooshed through my door, all energy and light, the Chi has been flowing, abundance abounds, and yes, I am pregnant!

Now, you ask, do I honestly believe there was a Buddha being whispering words of divinations to my psyche? Hmm.... Do I believe that it was Jami who single handedly reversed our lot? Hmm.... Would I do it all again? In an ultrasound heartbeat.

Thank you Great Spirit, thank you for Jami, and her innovative, powerful Earth Designs.

Ellen Drury Whitehurst

Earth Design

THE ADDED DIMENSION

Jami Lin

Earth Design Incorporated, Literary Division
Miami, Florida

Earth De/ign The Added Dimension
Published by: Earth Design, Incorporated
Copyright ©1995 by Earth Design, Incorporated

99 98 97 96 95   1 2 3 4 5 6

ISBN: 0-9643060-9-3

Earth Design is registered in the U. S. Patent and Trademark Office

For information:
Earth Design, Incorporated, Literary Division
P.O. Box 530725
Miami Shores, Florida 33138
Tel: (305) 756-6426
Fax: (305) 751-9995

Cover Design: Jami Lin, Wilfredo Agurto
Art Work: Wilfredo Agurto, Ardis Heiman, Jami Lin
Editor: Rita Lewison-Singer, Layna Fischer

Publisher's Cataloging-in-Publication

Earth Design: The Added Dimension/Jami Lin
          p.   cm.
Includes bibliographical references and index

        1. Interior Decoration. 2. Home furnishings. 3. Feng-Shui.
        4. Spiritual Direction. I. Title

TX315.l55 1994   747-dc20

To my friends, clients and teachers.

A Special Thanks to My Family: I Love You!

Joel Alan Levy

Ardis Heiman

Nana and Honey

I couldn't have done it without you!

Rita Lewison-Singer
Layna Fischer
Wilfredo Agurto

Thanks for your help!

Mitzie and Eddy Levy, Art and Susan Rochlin, Ranzi Vallecorse, Silk Waters, Lori Hodges, William Myran Friedman, Kathy Tumson, Lance Stelzer, Elizabeth Pierra, Tag and Judith Powell, Christina Roadruck, Betsy Lampe, Nancy Garcia and the Jazzerwomen, and Richard Nelson.

Disclaimer

The purpose of this manual is to educate and entertain. The author and Earth Design Incorporated, shall have neither liability nor responsibility to any person or entity with respect to any loss or damage caused, or alleged to be caused, directly or indirectly by the information contained in this book.

The wise man looks into space and does
not regard the small as too little nor
the great as too big, for he knows
there is no limit to dimensions.

Lao Tzu

Contents Wheel

Part One

THE FOUNDATION
Background and History

Part Two

STRUCTURE and SYSTEMS
The Methods

Part Three

THE TOP FLOOR
Personal Cultivation

"If there is harmony in the house, there is order in the nation. If there is order in the nation, there will be peace in the world."

An old Chinese proverb

Introduction

A few years ago, as I was hiking in the Canadian Rockies, I suddenly came to a realization; I had read many books about spiritual development, and in none of them had the authors ever committed to having been enlightened, even on the last page! Since college, I have known that I was supposed to synthesize information for the global good, and the *revelation on the mountain* took the pressure off! The subtlety of this insight gave me freedom to appreciate the magic of my daily experience and to explore the work to be done.

As a licensed interior designer with over fifteen years of practical field experience, I had been searching for a tool to combine my interest in metaphysics with my professional design expertise. When I asked the universe to link what I had originally considered to be very different subjects, the answers were presented to me.

Like the work of Joseph Campbell, who recognized that all cross-cultural mythologies had a similar universal spirit, my investigation identified a thread, as old as human evolution, linking the way we create our environments.

Analogous to mythology from ancient times to the present, Earth Design is a practical approach to man-made structures that blends science, design, creativity, and the universal spirit. The Earth Design combination can make a real difference in the human experience.

The purpose of this book is to add a missing dimension to your contemporary lifestyle. By adapting universal ideas and providing user-friendly design concepts, I will show you how to have a nicer looking home and office, along with greater harmony in your life. You will see that through the practical application of Earth Design concepts, buildings and their interiors can be harmonized with nature, thereby encouraging greater health, prosperity, and well-being for their occupants.

It is my intention to present ideas and concepts that are easily understood, so an individual who would ordinarily pick up a decorating ideas magazine can improve existing conditions or make inexpensive adjustments. However, the information is complete enough to inspire an architectural design professional to develop buildings based upon universal geometry and ecologically beneficial, non-toxic materials.

Part One provides a foundation to *ground* Earth Design by definition, history, science, and cross-cultural practices, and to establish its credibility. This will enable those readers who may be uncomfortable or unfamiliar with mystical concepts to alleviate their concerns.

The spiritual aspects of Earth Design are an integral part of the foundation and cannot be separated from the historic and scientific references. Through this integration and validation, you are invited to acknowledge that the universal spirit exists within each of us.

It is my intention to further awaken and provide you with the opportunity for deeper self discovery, which will inevitably enhance your well-being through a stronger connection of your mind, body, and spirit.

As the techniques and ideas are presented in Part Two, you will have a greater appreciation for the sources, the principles and how they can enhance your environment and your life. By utilizing the techniques and skills the same way ancient and contemporary designers have done, you will have better intuitive insight for applying Earth Design principles.

Part Three brings you full circle to observe Earth Design as a life process that explores natural law while perpetuating human spirit. Living and working surrounded by an aesthetically harmonized environment enables you to physically and emotionally experience the effects of Earth Design because you are living in greater grace.

Due to the memory of the design process within yourself and your physical environment, you have made a subconscious commitment to higher spiritual development. Earth Design is a tangible tool of expression which helps you maintain that connection. You can experience life as a happier being in the totality of all that you are becoming.

Most importantly, Earth Design connects your personal spirit to the Spirit of the Earth, and you become a link in planetary evolution. Through this connection, the momentum of spiritual humanness can perpetuate a loving global environment to share with future generations.

In love and light for global transformation . . .

Part One

THE FOUNDATION
Background and History

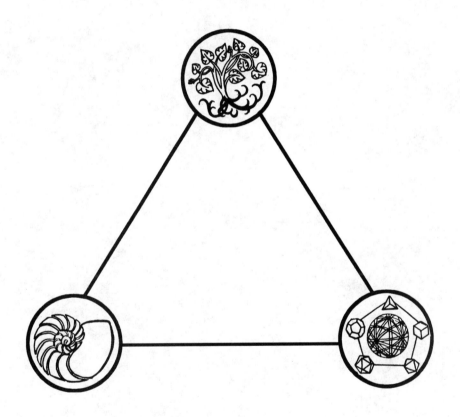

"And the seasons they go round and round
And the painted ponies go up and down
We're captive on a carousel of time
We can't return we can only look behind
From where we came
And go round and round
In the circle game." [a]

Joni Mitchell

Natural Law

In mid-February, the hazy sky reminds us that it is winter. Isn't it comforting to know that the budding life of spring is just around the corner? The ebb and flow of life tells the perpetuating story of the natural cycles. There is order and harmony.

Native Americans, the *earth people* of our land, use the words *Mi Ta Kuye Oyasin; All My Relations,* to describe the magical integration. *All is connected, and everything is sacred.* Take only what you need with respect and appreciation.

Gaia, the ancient name for the Earth, is a living entity with intent. Gaia has a soul and feelings. It is believed that many of her bodily functions are similar to our own involuntary circulatory system. The blood of the earth is the energy that flows throughout the universe and surrounds us, providing the momentum of sustained life.

As human beings, our connection to the cycles links us to the natural laws and to the rest of the universe. We are not merely living on the planet, we are an integral part of the living earth.

Our world has become so technologically advanced in the past several decades that we have forgotten how to recognize this sacred relationship. We are losing the ability to be in touch with the natural cycles and the forces of nature. Perhaps it is Gaia's purposeful intent, responding to our insensitivity, that has caused such recent natural disasters as hurricanes, floods, and earthquakes.

Gaia is asking us to take notice and help her to heal and preserve human existence. She knows that when nature is destroyed, our own human nature is also destroyed.

Without preservation, conservation, and regeneration of the earth's natural resources, we would not have a place to live! So let us evolve into earth-nurturing beings to enhance our personal lives and our environments as we move into the future.

The honor of our attention is no longer requested; it is now required!

Through Earth Design, our global awareness harmonizes with the natural laws and provides a closer relationship to the universal whole. Within the framework of our contemporary lifestyles, the renewed practices of ecological conservation, greater sensitivity, and spiritual awakening will bring abundance and transform ourselves on a global level. This interconnectedness will enhance even the way we treat each other as individuals.

To fulfill our destiny, we need to expect and accept greater health, harmony, and prosperity. When we choose to have maximum abundance in our lives, we live in harmony with the natural flow. We are like a tree that produces the optimum amount of fruit when it has the proper amount of light, water, and food.

The balance of nature can be viewed on both *micro* and *macro* levels. The micro reveals a cycle specific to itself, while the macro cycle is integral to the many other micro cycles. We recognize the snowball cause-and-effect of the food chain when an animal is no longer present in any given environment. For example, when animals who eat insects are no longer present in an environment, the locust implication may have plague-like proportions. Nature's balance shows us clearly why our existence is relevant to life on earth.

Can you recall your elementary science class? Think about the micro cycle of a seed, how it grows into a tree, shares itself as food, and flowers to produce new seeds. The tree has even greater regenerative properties in the macro cycle. It is also in harmony with the four basic elements: *air, water, fire* and *earth.* These elements are critical to all living things and will be an integral part of your study of Earth Design.

Air: The tree uses carbon dioxide and combines with the energy of the sun to produce chlorophyll for food, which in turn, provides us with fresh oxygen.

> *I'll never forget an experience in Athens, Greece. The air was so polluted with car exhaust that it was oppressive to breathe. I was sadden to experience ancient Greek "Earth Design" blackened and decayed by pollution. My first few steps into a lush park in the heart of Athens made a noticeable difference. There was a clearly defined line of fresh air where the trees and vegetation had purified the area.*

What cycles have you seen that made a heart-felt impression on you? Why was it important for you to take notice? What was the lesson? How can this sensitivity be applied to life? How does this experience relate to Earth Design?

The Lessons: Be observant to the cycles!
What can they teach?

Water: The tree is nourished by the rain, which helps it grow. By the tree's fruit, leaves, or seeds, we are nourished and return the water back to the earth. The water is purified through its percolation. It returns through evaporation and is recycled as snow and rain.

Earth: The tree gives throughout its life and also in its death. New life is generated from the organic nutrients produced as it decomposes in the earth.

> *On a hike in the Canadian Rockies, I observed grandfather tree had been dead for a long time. It had given its soft edible interior to the forest creatures as they helped the decaying processes. The tree was covered with luscious moss, and out of the stump, a proud baby tree was flourishing.*

Fire: Natural forest fires help in the micro life cycle of trees. A fire may force a seed pod to open, be transported by the *air*, and dropped to the *earth* to be sprouted and nurtured by *water*. Fire may also return a tree to the earth by producing ash.

Fire is also part of the macro life cycle of forests. Older trees often grow so tall that their leaf canopies block the light and prevent the growth of smaller vegetation. In turn, food is not produced to feed the smaller animals, to feed the larger animals, and so on. The National Park Service often allows controlled natural fires to burn which lets forests to regenerate and solve the imbalance.

As you can see, it is difficult, if not impossible, to discuss a tree's relationship to one of the four elements without mentioning the other related cycles. Everything in nature is harmoniously intertwined.

If you turn your attention to ecology, you realize that when a micro cycle is out of balance, the macro cycle is also affected. For example, too much fluorocarbon in the air creates a hole in the ozone, thus producing global warming and atmospheric earth changes.

Johnson Canyon:

> *At Lake Louise in the Canadian Rockies, I hiked through a narrow, thousand-foot deep canyon carved over the centuries by running water. A mature tree, perhaps 20 years old, had grown right out of a crack in the cliff face. As evidenced by the ninety-degree bend in the trunk, it had first started growing straight out of the vertical elevation. Knowing that the tree would break if it continued to grow perpendicular to the canyon caused it instinctively, intuitively, and with full intent to grow straight up.*

There are many lessons here:

Anything is possible when energy is added, including water cutting through 1,000 feet of solid rock.

There is a natural law of instinctive self-preservation, or spiritual energy, needed to be cultivated for growth.

Through our will and desire to solve problems, we need to grow and be flexible, like the tree, so our trunk will not break.

Our tenacity and persistence will allow us to succeed in what may appear to be an impossible situation or circumstance.

Earth Design is a multi-leveled study. Be flexible. There are personal discovery lessons everywhere in nature that enable your sensitivity and intuition to grow. Take time to reflect upon similar experiences. Your Earth Design and living abilities will be exponentially strengthened, and all aspects of your life will be more fun!

The Road to Hana:

> *On Maui in Hawaii, there is a long twisting road through the mountains leading to Hana. My husband Joel and I were advised that the drive was steep and difficult, so we decided to get up very early to spend the day. At 5:00 a.m., while it was still very dark, we began our trip. Four hours later, we arrived at a post office and a lovely hotel. That was Hana!*

The Lesson:

> *We were so anxious to get there that we missed the beautiful majesty of the Maui coast. We really were in the dark!*

It is the experience that counts, not the arrival. At the end of the road, the trip is *over*. At the end of your life, it is over too! Did you celebrate the moment? Were you sensitive to it, and what did you learn from the experience? Did you neglect to notice anything? Did you forget to live?

The Bug Lesson:

> *I encountered my first earthworm while bare-handedly digging in the backyard. Yuck, what a surprise! I didn't expect them to feel so much like they look! Now that I am accustomed to them, they are delightful to me. I know they are aerating and creating fertile soil for healthy plants. They are food for the birds that fill the air with song. Worms are a treasure and an integral part of the good energy created in my backyard.*

The obvious lesson here is that you don't have to venture very far to experience good earth energy. Dorothy, in *The Wizard of Oz*, simply clicked her magical red slippers and repeated,

"There is No Place like Home."
Dorothy was right!

You will learn how *home* supports you on all levels.

Examples of the relationship between nature and life are present everywhere; start paying attention to your experience and begin learning all over again. All these lessons will be assimilated in Earth Design because they ultimately affect the way you perceive and respond to the world.

Environment

According to *The World Book Dictionary*, environment is all of the surrounding conditions and influences that affect the development of a living thing. Included in this definition, the dictionary quotes from *Science News*, "Important as environmental factors are for shaping of human destiny, we now see clearly that man's influence on his environment, his controlled or uncontrolled behavior, are no less important than is the environment."

Environment, just like food and clothing, is essential to existence. Your environment is not just shelter. No matter how technically advanced society may become, when environments are designed according to natural laws, your well-being is enhanced. The environment supports you the same way Gaia provides for everything on the planet.

Everything you encounter in your home or office has an effect on you. Through Earth Design, you will learn to perceive the environment as a living entity with multiple-level energetics.

Yin-Yang

No one culture simplifies the natural laws better than the Chinese. They define the way of life, or *all that is*, as *The Tao* (pronounced dow). Like the philosophy of our Native American brothers, Tao is the law of integration and natural balance. *Taoist* (dow-ist) tradition uses the natural laws as the foundation of all Chinese ideology. The Tao practice breathes the life of natural law into oriental medicine, alchemy, art, poetry, philosophy and Earth Design.

The Taoist interacting symbol of harmonic balance, called *Yin-Yang*, has become universally recognized. This ancient graphic clearly shows the *spinning wheel* of opposites.

Yin-Yang, is not only the name of the symbol, but the essence of harmonious balance. The polar opposites define the duality required for all life to exist: male/female, flora/fauna, dark/light, and *wind/water*.[1]

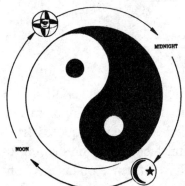

At midnight, there is an energy shift, and the night becomes day. At noon, we experience the polarity of day turning into night.

In each of the larger shapes there is a *dot* of the opposite. Taoist thought teaches that to maintain balance, it is necessary for some of the opposing force to be found in the other. The representation of this dot signifies that without one, the other cannot exist.

Yin-Yang describes the circle of life. Everything that exists can be simplified to this basic conceptual form. As the wheel spins, the macro and micro cycles of the natural laws maintain their balance.

---

[1]   Wind and water translates into *Feng Shui.*

Defined by the dictionary, *ecology* is a branch of biology that deals with the relationship of living things to their environment and to each other. Ever since people have lived on earth, we have ecologically tried to harvest and direct environmental forces [2] to improve the landscape, living conditions, and our lives. Thus, Earth Design is an *ecological art* that links humankind and our destiny with the surroundings.

Energy

Energy is the momentum of Yin-Yang. It is the glue that holds it all together. Energy moves; it flows; it can be felt. In high school science class, we were taught everything that exists is composed of molecular units called atoms. Atoms consist of dancing positive and negative charged energy particles. Positive/negative, male/female, fire/water, heaven/earth are balanced Yin/Yang energies.

The flow of energy in Earth Design applies the Chinese Yin-Yang theory of balance. Like the blood that circulates through our veins and nourishes our bodies, *Chi* [3] (pronounced chee or ki), is the Chinese word for energy.

Chi comes up from the earth core and circles the globe. Chi/energy is so powerful that it has the capacity to generate and destroy continents through tectonic plate and land mass movement.

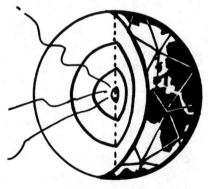

The natural laws of energy that create mountains are no different from Chi developed on a personal level. We need to develop our sensitivity to use and direct the energy in our bodies and environments.

---

[2]   Don't we harness *wind* and *water* to produce other types of energy such as electricity?

[3]   The words *energy* and *Chi* will be used synonymously throughout the text.

The flow of Chi is the most important aspect of Earth Design to understand because it defines:

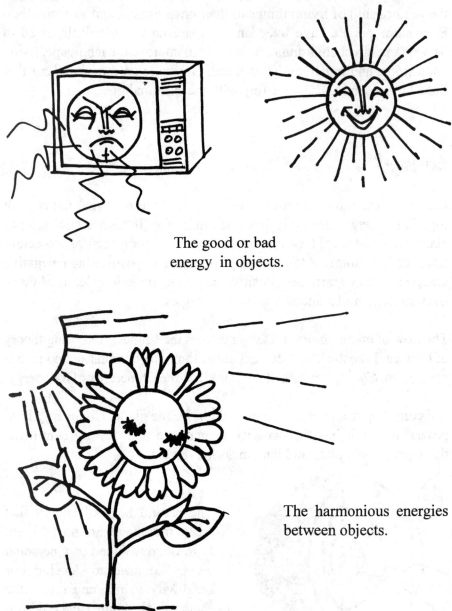

The good or bad
energy in objects.

The harmonious energies
between objects.

Chi is the life force that circulates in your body, home, and office. It is your personal and environmental Chi that will nourish your ability to receive optimum health, harmony, creativity and prosperity.

"It is now known everything gives off certain types of
energies and that the entire earth has an electromagnetic
field with variations from place to place which are
significant enough to influence the health and behavior of
living things." [b]

Initially, you need to understand the existing energetics of natural or
man-made conditions before you begin the Earth Design process. You
can then observe the situation and make aesthetic decisions that affect
your environmental and personal Chi. Ultimately, through developed
intuition, common sense, and understanding the practices, you can make
the appropriate energetic modifications. By arranging your rooms,
furniture, and accessories in a certain way, you will be in harmony with
the natural laws.

**Earth Design is a process, so get your creative juices flowing.
However, the process has many dimensions, and it is best to finish
the book before you make financial decisions regarding your Earth
Design project.**

Scientific, physiological, genetic, and environmental studies have
examined personal energetics. Twins separated at birth and living under
different environmental conditions were found to have very similar
energetics. These studies determined that both environmental and
lifestyle variations make a difference in personal energetics and have a
major affect on us.

Because Chi is different in each person, place, and thing, you will learn
to modify the energies for the proper balance and for your maximum
benefit. You will learn how to evaluate personal Chi and combine it with
environmental energetics.

Chi flow

The easiest way to experience Chi is in your body with the power surge of exercise. Your heart rate goes up, and your body physically gets hot. However, energy is still present while your body is at rest because it is the source that drives your involuntary systems.

Exercise: *Experience the energy for yourself. Rub your hands together and feel the heat caused by the friction. Move your hands further apart, then closer together. Be sensitive to the varying degrees of heat you feel between your hands. You are experiencing your own Chi energy field.*

Proper Chi flow in your environment is similar to drinking a glass of water. When you drink the water, it nourishes, refreshes, cleanses, and gives you vitality as it moves through your body. After you receive the benefits, the water moves on. It follows the most efficiently designed path in your body to obtain the maximum value.

The path of Chi can also nourish, refresh, cleanse, and vitalize your space. When Chi is blocked, it will have limited beneficial effect.

Recognition of the paths of proper Chi flow is the one of the main principles of Earth Design.

Learn to visualize energy as it moves through space. This architectural *flow diagram* [c] is used to analyze energy movement.

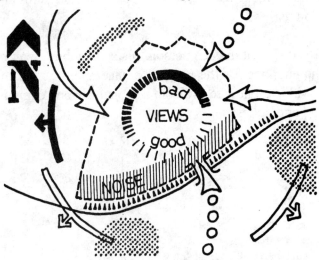

It was exciting to realize that the drawings I did in architecture school showed how Chi moves through space. However, while I was learning to use dimension and scale, I wasn't made aware of the *Added Dimension of Chi Life Force!* This awareness is my contribution to design evolution through Earth Design. Chi is the healing energy of our design; it is the breath that enhances our environments.

There is an exciting relationship between Interior and Earth Design.

Traditional flow diagrams are graphic representations of such various movement considerations as: air circulation from nature or air-conditioning systems, sun orientation and its movement during the day, vehicular or pedestrian traffic flow, or how much light hits certain surfaces.

The easiest energies to recognize are the ones you can experience through your five senses. By understanding *tangible energy,* you will later see how you can also apply the same principles to the intangible, unseen, and subconscious energies.

Problem 1:

What if the design of the roof overhang or windows does not protect the house with a direct western exposure from tremendous heat loads in the late afternoon?

Problem 2:

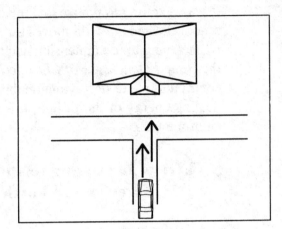

This house is being bombarded with *Sha* or negative energy from the oncoming car traffic. The house may be located at the end of a long street, a bridge, or at the bottom of a hill. The occupants will feel the effect of Sha from the cars.

Most design problems may be solved both physically and energetically. When you recognize the effect of the energy, you can make the physical adjustments.

You can make your surroundings more beautiful and align your environment to the natural laws at the same time.

Solution 1:

Plant shrubs in proportion to the angle of the sun to block the heat from coming in the windows.

When a heat problem occurs in a high rise, it is best to tint your windows or consider some kind of window treatment. *Blackout shades* reflect and hold the heat between the window and fabric.

Personally, I am not fond of blackouts because they obstruct natural light and Chi flow. I only use them for clients that request a blackened bedroom or for an office presentation room where slides or videos are shown.

My favorite solution for window treatments is translucent shades that you can see through during the day, while allowing natural light and Chi to flow. These shades come in many colors and have a silver solar back. The back reflects 80% of the heat and ultraviolet rays, which also reduces fading on furnishings and textiles.

You can always add an appropriate decorative treatment on top of the shade if it adds to the decor. Be careful: if you can see through the shades during the day, your neighbors can also see through them when your lights are on at night.

Solution 2:

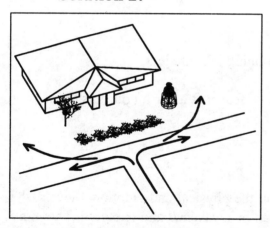

Plant shrubs so they will grow into a dense hedge and deflect Sha, or in a front garden, position several large rocks toward the direction of oncoming cars to energetically solve the problem.

When you are considering solutions, always make sure they are harmonious and in energetic balance with surrounding conditions. Are the plants in proportion to the rest of the landscape?

Make sure there is plenty of pedestrian area by the doors. Keep in mind how the plants will look from the windows while you are standing inside. They must not be planted too close to the window because they could potentially overpower it and prevent natural light or Chi from entering.

Energy movement can be beneficial or detrimental, depending upon the kind of energy it is and if it is moving at the proper speed. As you saw in Problem 1, the sun energy, which is typically beneficial, was unfavorable because the room got too hot. We were, however, able to adjust the situation into a favorable condition.

While we were not able to control the oncoming traffic in Problem 2, we could deflect the negative energy from the cars away from the house.

As you have seen in the examples, it is easy to recognize the benefits:

On a physical level---

Solution 1: The space is more comfortable because there is less heat and glare.

Solution 2: You enjoy the plants, which block the vista of cars zooming toward your house, and traffic noise is absorbed.

On an emotional level---

Solution 1: Your air-conditioning bills are less.

Solution 2: The subconscious fear that a car might crash into your house is gone.

On a spiritual level---

When you are more at ease on the physical and emotional levels, the spiritual aspects of yourself can be awakened and explored. The more conscious you are about the spiritual aspects of yourself, the greater the experience on the other levels. Even without spiritual consciousness, when you enhance the energetics of a space, your subconscious mind still recognizes the benefits.

**Earth Design solutions are experienced
on all levels!**

By practicing Earth Design, you participate in the natural cycles while enjoying the beauty and energetic benefits of plants. You also nurture the earth, reduce soil erosion, add organic material to the soil when the leaves drop, and help to recycle carbon dioxide into oxygen.

Keep your foliage healthy and trimmed so as not to obstruct walkways, doors, or windows. When you have healthy shrubs, birds and animals grace your environment, which is further confirmation of beneficial Chi.

Even if a design solution doesn't include plants, by the very nature of earth sensitivity, you will want to practice good ecological and conservation habits. Because personal development of Chi is essential to Earth Design, you will also learn to recognize the spiritual aspects of the earth. By experiencing earth energy, you will understand the momentum of the natural cycles. By practicing Earth Design, you become physically, emotionally, and spiritually connected to the wholeness of the universe.

Catch 69!

This magical connection with and to the natural laws is the cyclical momentum that I call *Catch 69!* because the Yin-Yang symbol looks like the number 69.

Catch 69! [4] is the positive polarity of the negative *Catch 22*. Catch 22 describes a cycle that leads nowhere, and you cannot get out. Life becomes like the Greek myth of Sisyphus, who spent eternity rolling a rock up a hill but never reached the top. Or in more modern terms, you don't like your boss, so you don't give 110 percent to your job, so you never get a raise, so you don't like your boss, and around and around you go.

---

[4]   The sexual connotation that arises from this image also fits within my definition of Catch 69! From Taoist, Native American, and other traditions, sexual energy or the harmonics between male and female energy are the momentum of creation. A seedling would never have an opportunity for growth if masculine pollen hadn't fertilized the feminine seed.

Catch 69! follows the principles of Earth Design. When your environments are physically enhanced, your emotional body is strengthened, which activates your spirit. The cycle repeats when your spirit energizes the ability to use intuition, which helps you make better physical Earth Design decisions. When you work on spirit, through whatever path, it perpetuates greater abundance.

On what carousel do you want to ride?

The best part of Catch 69! is that you become a perpetual spinning wheel. It is your micro cycle for inner peace and happiness. Because of natural law, we do not live independently from each other. The dots or voids in the Yin-Yang represent the other people in our lives.

As a spinning wheel, when you interact with your family, friends, and acquaintances, the *voids* within you become filled and you become *whole*. Then, as a whole being, through the macro cycle, you fill the voids in the people you contact. Their subconscious minds respond to their own spiritual needs as they too begin to spin and develop.

As more of us *catch* the Yin-Yang cycle of personal development, we make an impact on the rest of the world. The beauty of our well-designed earth will be appreciated, and the human experience will be enhanced.

Catch 69! Is Evolution.
Personal and Global: Physical, Emotional and Spiritual.

**Apply Earth Design to add your spirit to your environment.
Harmonize with the natural laws and be in harmony within yourself.**

Get caught in Catch 69! It feels so good. Sharing adds the missing dimension and fills the void in our spinning wheels. Catch 69! is wonderfully addictive.

Meditation:

Close your eyes. Center and relax yourself by taking a few slow, deep, concentrated breaths. Visualize masculine sun energy as a gold light coming down through the top of your head and feminine earth energy as silver light coming up from the ground through the bottoms of your feet. Visualize these energetic lights filling every cell in your body as they meet at your heart, creating a spinning wheel of white light. Expand this protective and nurturing light to form a bubble that surrounds your body.

Now, with the Catch 69! light around you, imagine the events of your day. What happens when you talk to your children, how does your boss respond to you, what happens in the grocery store? Experience your light touching people with kindness and sensitivity. Watch them soften as you become happier fulfilling your tasks.

As you complete each interaction in your mind's eye, mentally thank the other people for your experience with them, and give them some of your light.

Make a commitment to share your light during the actual experiences you have each day. Thank yourself for taking these few minutes. Then, when you are ready, bring your awareness back into the room and open your eyes.

Before going to sleep, review the actual experiences of your day. Was your energetic white light around you? Did it make a difference in the way you perceived the world? Did it make a difference in your attitude and in the responses of others? Did this energetic make you happier?

So what is Earth Design?

Earth Design incorporates all the principles of natural law. It is a simple name for the applications that combine the new and ancient sciences, the cycles of nature, spirit and mysticism, personal observations, and conventional interior design.

Earth Design adds another dimension to our lives through affirming our purposeful connection to Gaia. To be in alignment is personally rewarding because you learn to reap the fruit of abundance. To be an Earth Designer, you become spiritually sensitive as you make the connection to the energies the same way the earth's ancient people understood them.

"The idea of a sacred place where the walls and laws of the temporal world dissolve to reveal wonder is apparently as old as the human race." [a]

Joseph Campbell

Historical Geomancy

Geomancy is *Earth Geometry*. The words *geometry* and *geomancy* are derived from the ancient Greek words: *geo* meaning *Gaia* or *earth*, *metry* meaning *to measure*, and *mancy* translates into *mantos,* which means *to divine, of spirit.* Geomancy is the law of balance and proportion combined with the spirit or energy that connects all form.

Geomancy is the practice of using inherent energy to live in harmony with the earth. Earth Design is a synthesis of geomancy, conventional aesthetic design, and personal divination. Geomancy is one form of divination.[1]

---

[1]   In addition to practices that specifically relate to geomancy, there are many others that are complex studies in themselves. Briefly, ancient practices include: the Shamans, Seers or Medicine Men of Siberia, Mexico, North, Central and South America (including the United States), Japan, Tibet, Indonesia, Aboriginal Australia, and Nepal.

There is the divination of the Celtics of Wales, Scotland, Ireland, and Brittany that threw the Ogam sticks. There are the ancients of the Germanic world that threw the

Through educated interpretation and intuition, divination enables choice of action rather than dogmatic prediction. Like Earth Design, geomancy is used to maintain the natural flow of the earth while incorporating that vital life energy into our environments and bodies.

Geomancy is the energy or *Soul of Mother Earth.* By living at one with the earth, ancient geomancers understood that by preserving the *Earth Spirit,* abundance, well-being, and a full life were attainable. By definition, geomancy has been a major factor in all historical design and architecture. "Geomancy may be described as an ancient, holistic, integrated system of natural science and philosophy, used to keep human activity in harmony with natural patterns: from seasonal cycles, to processes that maintain the balance of nature, to the geometrical proportions found in the way all organisms grow." [b]

Geomantic practices are as ancient and culturally diverse as are the roots of language. The integration of natural science and spirit and their connection to the environment have been interpreted in many ways and have universal similarities.

The basic tenet of geomancy comes from the realm of spirit. When our lives are postured in connection with our inner spirit, the flow of purpose is engaged. Instinctively, this connection forms the basis of philosophies, for which the ancients generated stories of symbolism and creation.

Runes, the reading of the bones in Southern Africa, Chinese casting of the Hexagrams in the *I Ching,* and through Kaballastic tradition, Tarot cards are read.

There is gazing into crystal balls or dark pools of water, tea-leaf reading, palmistry, reading dreams, and numerology (from the Kaballah, *I Ching,* and the Verdic Square).

There are new divination practices on the market, as a different medicine card can be pulled for various readings. I have even seen Pleiadian symbols drawn on sea shells that were used for divining.

The natural laws have had a major influence on all the above divination practices, and because shelter is one of our basic needs, they most likely are linked to geomancy.

The stories were explanations about the workings of nature. Myths, created by the ancient soul, were symbols of natural laws and the relationship of heaven and earth. Many myths provided instructions, which developed into ritualistic action and created cultural order. Some myths regarded the ability to consult with individuals that had divine powers. Through ritual, the seers provided guidance, advice, and faith because of their special connection to spirit.

Seers would often reside in selected sites that had special energy and mystical powers. Cross-culturally, *geo-mythology* tells stories of the earth and sacred space. These stories either provide information that defines the sacredness of a site or instructions for ceremonies and rituals performed there.

When myths described the sacredness of a site, they often suggested that these locations were only to be used as the gods' earthly home. Many of these locations are still used today as places of worship. Native Americans would never consider using a sacred mountain to make camp, just as we would not have a party inside a church.

Myth defined such sacred space as Delphi, Greece, where the Oracle of Apollo, home of the Greek Sun God, is located.

> This site is one of the most magical Temples of God that I have experienced. From the power, energy, and natural beauty, it was obvious to me why the ancient Greeks selected this location. *I was able to feel my own spiritual connection with the site and to the ancient stories.*

Delphi, according to mythology and anthropological documentation, developed into a great religious center. Prophetic consultations were used for such personal undertakings as getting married or taking journeys. This guidance was important throughout ancient Greek life and is mentioned in many myths. Even the great Socrates was said to have consulted the Oracle.

There are several common factors beyond energetic beauty that many sacred locations share:

> Delphi, for example, is nestled in the *classic geomantic site configuration*. The mountain behind it protects the site from the north wind, the one to the right protects against the hot western sun, and the one to the left balances the height of the mountain on the right. The front of the site provides an open view to give the inhabitants warning in the event of any intrusion, and the river Pleistos provides nurturing Chi, water, and food for the site.

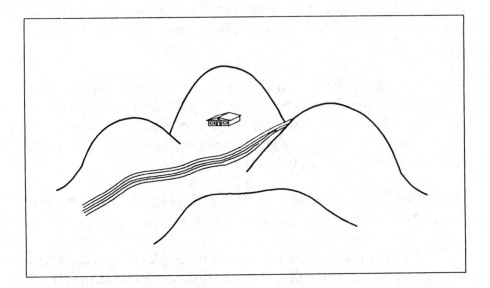

This topographical layout has also been described by Chinese geomancers as the perfect site configuration. It has been mythologicalized by the animal representations of the cardinal directions: The Chinese describe the Black Tortoise of the north, the Green Dragon to the east, the Red Phoenix to the south, and the White Tiger to the west.[2]

Neither the Greeks nor the Chinese have an exclusive on this layout. This geomantic configuration is universal in scope. The ancients selected sites

---

[2]   It is interesting to note that the Chinese often used *Warrior* instead of Tortoise to define the energy of the north. *Native American* Warriors by definition are seekers of truth that mythologically describe the North American continent as Turtle Island.

though logic and intuition. Likened to being wrapped in your mother's arms, when a site is wrapped in the paws of these *sacred animals*, there is natural protection from the elements.

Native Americans regularly sought out these protective sites. In New Mexico, at the Taos Pueblo, there is a tribe nestled in this configuration and living there the same way they did over one thousand years ago. Anasazi Indian sites throughout the southwestern United States, such as the cliff dwellers at Bandelier by Los Almos, New Mexico, are located with the same orientation.

There is a purposeful selection of the site relative to where it is positioned on earth. Many sacred sites were used as geographic markers. Delphi is located directly on a latitude line. The Oracles of Dodona and Delos are each one latitude away on either side of Delphi and appear to define a mapping system.

Recent studies have theorized, "The original purpose of the oracle sites was connected with a reverence for the earth spirit, and the meticulous measurements were not merely for navigational purposes, but for explaining the deep mysteries of the measurement of the Earth as a sphere and cosmic motions, which to the ancients were the profoundest mysteries of all. As the centuries wore on, however, the oracles achieved increasing prominence and the geodetic function was forgotten."[c]

In Judeo-Christian ideology, geo-mythology and geomancy are found in The Bible. *Exodus 36-40* describes specific detailed instructions for the construction of the Tabernacle.[3] The text describes *millwork drawings* that include complete dimensions, construction materials, and ornamentation. The *specifications* describe in detail the length, number of fabric panels, and the colors of the curtains.

Geo-mythology and geomancy are not limited to the ancient cultures mentioned above. Universal earth symbols were used in all forms of geomancy. Symbols of the Earth Goddess are used in Shamanic traditions. Even earth itself is used in Navaho and Tibetan healing

---

[3]   The Tabernacle is the building where Hebrews worshiped and still do.

ceremonies through sand paintings. Earth is symbolically used in Earth Design through Chinese and Western Astrological geomantic interpretations.

Earth Design is the blending of ancient geomancy and geo-mythological practices with our contemporary lives. Our own mythology is the combination of personal history, relationships, dreams, and the ceremonies we create for such life events as the anticipation of birth, childhood play, holidays, and the memory of loved ones.

Stories that remind us of universal concepts such as, **"There really *is* no place like home,"** define us as spiritual beings. "We have an inner geometry in our bodies and an inner biology, which becomes an extension of our planet/world, making our bodies and the planet interchangeable. We reflect what is 'out there' because it is within us, and because it is in us, we see it out there."[d]

Historical Geomancers and Scientists

Being able to recognize relationships between the earth and the heavens made historical geomancers natural scientists as well. It is hard to differentiate between the professions. Both have made their discoveries by observing the harmonics of natural relationships.

Unlike modern scientists, however, early scientists did not limit their perceptions to what could be proven. Their theories were based on the integral workings of the universe. Discoveries were made through the relationships between growth cycles and mathematics.

These natural science geomancers have been around since recorded history. **Pythagoras**, who lived between 582-507 BC, "created a humanistic philosophy which used mathematical harmony and proportion as primary tools in daily life, including art, architecture, music,[4] and history. He believed that the order inherent in numbers, a number

---

[4] According to Pythagoras, the *music of the spheres* is the harmonious movement of the planets, mathematically expressed, corresponding to numbers representing harmonic musical sounds.

symbolism, creates specific effects on the observer, both psychologically and spiritually."[e] As humans are an integral part of the natural cycle, Pythagoras added humanitarian factors to his scientific discovery. He understood that this humanitarian philosophy incorporates human spirit because it energizes the deepest core of our subconscious.

From your high school geometry class, do you remember the *Pythagorean Theorem?* This formula of triangles, more than 2,500 years old, is one of the basic laws of geomancy. Triangles are repeated through archetypal symbolism, sacred shapes, architecture, natural science, and Earth Design.

Plato, who lived between 427-347 BC, "believed the world to be ordered by divine intelligence according to the laws of symmetry."[f] He discovered five geometrical solid shapes[5] that would fit, with all their apexes touching, inside a sphere. He identified the *Platonic Solids* through the sequence of natural numbers and the *five elements,*[6] which defined the structure of the universe.

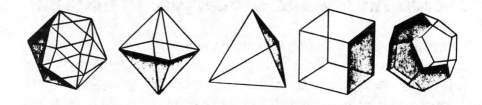

---

[5] Interestingly, there are carved stones about 2 ½ inches in diameter, dating from 1200 BC, found in Scotland and Britain. These stones, carved 800 years before Plato, have the same precise measurements and shapes as the Solids. Anthropologists believe that these stones were used by the ancients to define geometries of the earth and the cosmos.

[6] We will refer to these five elements in Chapter 5, *Feng Shui.*

About two thousand years later, **Leonardo da Vinci** (1452-1519) and **Johannes Kepler** (1571-1630) discovered that everything in nature, including the human body, the earth, and the universe itself, may be broken down by the exact characteristic proportions of the Platonic Solids.

To further show geomancy in the cosmic order, Kepler recognized how the Platonic Solids defined the mathematics of the planetary orbits. He found "that when the solids are inscribed within the spheres, and within each other in sequence, the mathematics described the orbits of the planets in the solar system."[g]

What did the ancients in Britain and Scotland, Pythagoras, Plato, and Kepler have in common? From different periods, perspectives, and interests, there was a commonality ascribed to the order of things. Even the atom is defined by these universal shapes.

There are no *coincidences* in nature;
The universe is designed with a masterful purpose.

Sacred Shapes and Archetypal Symbolism

Symbolic shapes are archetypal graphic representations of the natural laws. They are used numerously through cross-cultural myth and philosophy, ancient art, religion, and such personal mythology as dreams. The shapes are included throughout ancient architecture, thereby adding humanistic, spiritual, and geomantic qualities to buildings.

For our purpose, when building an Earth Design foundation, it is necessary to understand the spiritual symbolism of some geomancy shapes. These shapes have archetypal characteristics that activate spiritual qualities within us.

Whether or not these symbols have conscious meaning for you, they are part of the collective unconscious, and therefore, a part of you. This framework justifies Earth Design, serves as historical reference, and helps you to integrate sacred symbolism into your design. When you consciously incorporate the symbols in your design, as did the ancients, your environment can become a personally supportive, sacred space.

The Universal Shapes

Circles/Spheres:

> Representative of one of the Platonic Solids, the circle signifies wholeness. It is the spinning wheel of natural law, without top or bottom, beginning or end. The circle is the Yin-Yang balance of polarity. Circles are representations of living entities. Living circles are the cycles of nature: the seasons, the heavenly bodies and their orbits and planetary phases, atoms, the cycles of life and death, and the energy center *chakras*[7] in our bodies. The Earth Sphere is a living circle.
>
> This recurring shape can be appreciated by observing such objects in nature as: ripples in a pond, a snowflake, the cross section of a tree, a sunflower, or by gazing into the eyes of a loved one.

Life Circles are tools of divination and geomancy used in the search for higher meaning and personal growth through connection to the spiritual whole. Often there are circles within circles that are symbolic of deep interconnection. Life circles are the tangible manifestation of the natural cycles represented by this sacred symbolism. Universal models are in geometric proportion and progression. Their nucleus is the unification of the universal soul or the collective consciousness. The soul has also been described as the collective consciousness by one of the pioneers of psychotherapy, Carl Gustav Jung.

A *mandala* is a life circle, literally translated from Sanskrit, it means circle or center. The center is symbolic of the eternal potential. The mandala is a "structural matrix through and from which flow a succession of changes, elemental forms, and primal surges, each surpassing the other

---

[7]   *Chakra* is the Sanskrit word for wheel. There are seven major chakras or energy centers in our body by which we process life energies.

in an infinite variety of organic structures and impulses, crowned by the supreme attribute of reflective consciousness. Its flow, working through a relatively well-defined structure, is subject to the infinite process of growth and transformation by virtue of the ever-changing relationships, both internal and external to its basic structure."[h]

Mandalas have been used cross-culturally throughout time as meditation tools. Jung used mandalas with his patients because he saw that they were powerful tools for self discovery.

Sometimes prayer mandalas are used as meditative tools for spiritual growth. Take a minute to enjoy the following excerpt from *Ezekiel's Vision* that comes from Judeo-Christian mythology:

Exercise:　　*Go to a quiet place; by reading the passage out loud, you will experience it through your mind's eye as it is reinforced by your ears. What do you see?*

"As I looked at the living creatures, I saw wheels on the ground, one beside the four. The wheels sparkled like topaz, and they were all alike: in form and working, they were like a wheel within a wheel, and when they moved in any of the four directions, they never swerved in their course. All had hubs, and each hub had a projection which had the power of sight, and the rims of the wheels were full of eyes all around. When the living creatures moved, the wheels moved beside them; when the creatures rose from the ground, the wheels rose; they moved in whatever direction the spirit would go; and the wheels rose together with them, for the spirit of the living creature was in the wheels. When the one moved, the other moved; when one halted, the other halted; when the creatures rose from the ground, the wheels rose together with them, for the spirit of the creatures was in the wheels."

*Did you see and experience the mandalas? Did you see your spirit in the mandala vision? Did you **experience** universal symbolism and its significance?*

Physical mandalas come in many different forms and sizes. Large mandalas are stone circles or medicine wheels used by native peoples. The ancients also used stone circles such as Stonehenge to measure terrestrial and astrological cycles. Mandalas are located in fine European gardens with their concentric circles of manicured hedges. Notice the maze on the floor at Chartres Cathedral is shaped with the same mandala design.

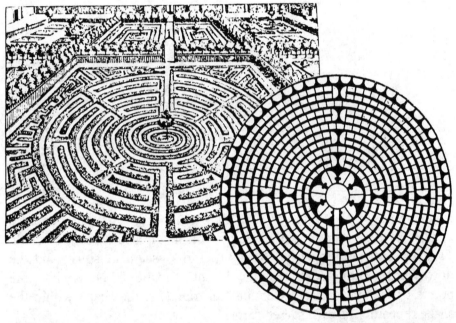

On a smaller scale, there are many graphic representations of the spiritual cycles, such as the Aztec Sunstone, Mayan Calendar, and our personal astrological chart. Mandalas at this scale are often artistic spiritual expressions of humanistic geomancy, like the previously mentioned Native American sand paintings and the Tibetan Wheels of Life.

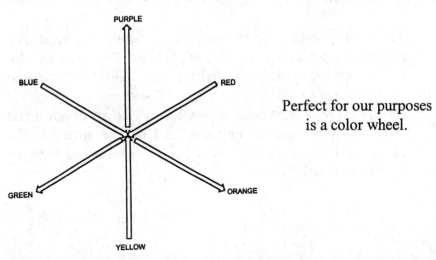

Perfect for our purposes is a color wheel.

Triangles and Pyramids:

The triangle has universal significance, represented by man's quest to ascend to the spiritual realms as the apex reaches toward the heavens. Representations include: the triad of physical and spiritual wholeness represented by the *Christ energy triad*: Father, Son, and Holy Spirit, or the mind, body, and spirit connection.

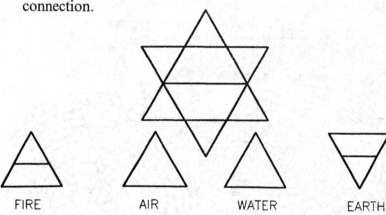

FIRE   AIR   WATER   EARTH

In the *Seal of Solomon*, or *Star of David*, the two interconnected equilateral triangles represent the four elements: fire, air, water, and earth. "The upward pointing triangle signifies the ascent of spirit, and the downward pointing triangle is the decent of matter." [i] Notice how the points of the star create six equilateral triangles; the shape within the shape repeating its own sacred form.

Additional shapes created by connecting triangles include the Platonic Solids, a circle (in two-dimension) and a sphere (in three-dimension).

Squares/Cubes:

The square is not a natural phenomenon; however, it is created by connecting two triangles by the hypotenuse. Squares were also created because of the humanitarian factor, or man's unconscious spiritual need for order and balance. "The square and circle are the harmonious balance of human and divine, of physical and spiritual worlds, and of imperfect and perfect qualities. The square and circle are metaphors for the equilibrium between heaven and earth."[j]

Spiral:

> The spiral shape suggests a deeper or higher knowing. It is symbolic of infinity as either an ascent or descent, depending on the inward or outward movement of the spiral.

The spiral is geometrically and geomantically proportioned like the Platonic solids. The spiral is the pattern of expansion based upon the *Golden Section, Golden Mean,* or *Phi,* which are mathematically found in many natural forms.

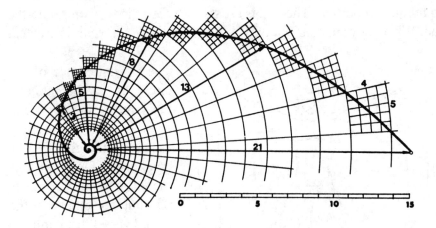

"Where these ratios occur, resonance with the natural patterns of growth and regeneration insures harmony and accord with the universal will. Therefore, geomancers, architects, and artists employ this cannon of proportion in the construction of temples and works of art."[k] This recurring modulation is present in the cross section of a nautilus shell, in the array of seeds of a sunflower, and in human body proportion. Spirals have been universally depicted throughout time, as seen in ancient Egyptian artifacts.[8]

---

[8]   How could the Egyptians even begin to fathom the double helix of the DNA molecule spiral as a basic building block of life?

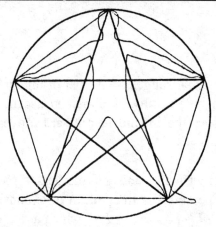

The famous illustration by Leonardo da Vinci graphically represents the mathematical symmetry of the Golden Section between the circle, square, and human proportion. The points are the two feet, the two arms, and the head. When they are connected by drawn lines, a *pentagram*[9] is created.

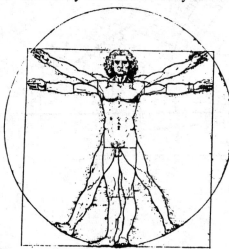

The circumference of the circle is mathematically the same as the perimeter of the square, thereby "squaring the circle." The humanistic factor of this sacred geometry defines the human body as the scared vessel that connects earth (square) and heavens (circle).

Man's sacred relationship to the heavens is further shown by the graphic, "Symbolic representation of man and the microcosms, through the astrological symbols of Mars, Jupiter, Saturn, Mercury, and Venus at the apexes of the pentagram."[1]

---

[9] *Coincidentally*, Pythagoras used the pentagram with Leo's Man as his emblem. Did you notice that Leonardo lived one-thousand years **after** Pythagoras?

Cross:

This symbol represents the energy of the four cardinal directions: north, south, east, and west. The cross is also a representation of the *four elements: water, fire, earth,* and *air.*

The cross is represented by the earthly manifestation of human incarnation, or Christ energy, as known by some traditions.

The Bagua:

The Bagua is a universal symbol that comes directly from the ancient Chinese text, *I Ching: The Book of Changes and the Unchanging Truth.* The historical symbolic representation defines harmonic inner workings of the natural energetics. The Bagua is represented by a series of eight tri-grams that are symbolically constructed out of graphic representations of Yin-Yang.

The Bagua is stylized on the front cover, and in the *Contents Wheel Mandala.* From an Earth Design perspective, the mandala is a universal symbol because it combines triangles to form a life circle. In Chapters 5 and 6, you will see how the Bagua refers to life situations and to the planetary cycles.

Geomancy in Application

Ancient structures, strategically located on sacred sites, were built according to archetypal geometry. By building according to the spiritual energy of geometric structure, the ancient architects deepened their personal connection to the universal collective.

The momentum of Catch 69!

> "Nature is deepened in the biology and geometry of our bodies. As we begin to connect with the places of spirit in our environment, through awareness we can begin to connect with places of spirit in our bodies."[m]

Earth Design unconsciously touches upon mythic dimensions of self and activates our higher spiritual qualities.

The parameters of location, architectural stability, integrity of form, and construction materials have been tested through the centuries by the spiritual humanistic factor. The Colosseum, the Pantheon, the Great Wall of China, the Parthenon, the Temple at Machu Pichu, Chichen Itza, the Egyptian Pyramids, and many others are still standing in all their power, grace, and beauty.

Why are they still available to us? What are their stories? How are they connected to spirit? Is this *coincidental*?

Earth Connections

Ancient architecture is a combination of many sacred shapes and structural form. The tent, one of the earliest structures designed by man, represents home design excellence. The tent solved the housing problems of migratory native peoples who followed their source of food.

The native peoples designed their tents by noticing that the triangular shape of a mountain was the most stable of structural forms. The narrowest part at the top had the least amount of wind resistance, and it grew in stability toward the base. In its simplicity, the tent was light enough to transport and easy to reassemble.

> *If you look at a tent in three-dimensions, isn't there a circular form at the base where it connects to the earth? Since you are in training to "see" like an Earth Designer, notice the mandala of concentric circles created by all the cross sections when cutting through the central axis.*

The Egyptians also recognized the triangular form. They believed the land was an integral part of the triad connection of earth, the cosmos, and human spirit. Even Egyptian topography reflected the concept of the pyramids through the sacred shape of the Nile delta. Theories suggest the Egyptians selected the pyramid shape because they subconsciously needed mountains in their landscape, perhaps to create a man-made classical site configuration.

Though the triad, the Egyptians understood that reality was incomplete without a connection to the spiritual realm. Through mythology and hieroglyphic language, the Egyptians delved into the conscious and subconscious mind for spiritual meaning. Spiritual life directly relates to mythology and pyramid construction. The pyramids contained mummified Pharaohs, which were said to preserve the Spirit of Osiris, necessary to sustain Egyptian life for all eternity.

The Egyptians understood that "the earth acts just like the human body in having subtle and gross energies crossing its surface and interior, and that blockages produce illness while a free flow of energy leads to health."[n] With this sensitivity, Egyptian structures were built with purpose through energetic flow, spirit, sacred dimension, harmonic proportion, and mythology. Because of all the factors that went into Egyptian design, Imhotep, the most renowned Egyptian architect, was also recognized as a priest, scholar, astrologer, magician, and medical healer.

While the Egyptians predated Plato and Pythagoras, Imhotep used the same mathematical proportions-and-ratios relationships. The proportion of 3:4:5, the Pythagorean ratio of a right angle triangle, is repeated throughout Egyptian sculpture and architecture.

Squaring the circle was used repeatedly. The Great Pyramid at Giza, *coincidentally* located in the apex of the Nile delta, is an example. When a circle is drawn to connect the points, on either the square of the plan view or the triangles of the elevation or section, the circumference of the circle is equal to the perimeter of the square.

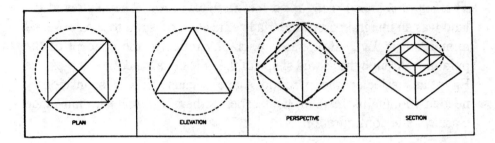

When the structures or design details are constructed according to universal geometry, a human will feel at home, whatever the size of a building. Not only is the proportion relative to natural law, but Leonardo's man reminds us that this proportion is symbolic of such humanitarian factors as the universal psyche and spirit of man.

Exercise: *Open your wallet, and pull out a one dollar bill. Look at the back. What comes to your mind's eye? As you look at the pyramid with the eye at the capital, what spirit is reaching toward the heavens?*

With these *mathematical coincidences,* the pyramids were not only constructed as burial chambers, they also served many other functions. The Great Pyramid at Giza, constructed for Pharaoh Cheops, marks the perfect longitude and latitude at the center of the world as the Egyptians knew it. It is also said that the Great Pyramid was used as a surveying instrument, initiation temple, astronomical observatory, telescope, and standard for systems, weights, and measures. The Great Pyramid, beautiful in its simplicity, is probably the oldest, most complex example of sacred geometry.

It is fascinating to think about the enduring symbolism of these Egyptian structures that are over 4,000 years old. From an architectural and structural perspective, no wonder the simple triangular shape, as in any building truss, is used in today's construction and materials.

Spirals:

The spiral shape is the geometric progression of Phi. The patterns of growth are represented as far back as Mayan civilization. The spiral is experienced in Mayan Temples with smaller and smaller levels as the pyramid shape reaches toward the heavens.

The sacred shape of infinity was clearly used in the award-winning Guggenheim Museum in New York City, designed by Frank Lloyd Wright. There is the constant flow of Chi in the stratified layers of the building. You can experience the symbolism of infinity as you move down the spiral pathway. Your eyes have no abrupt change, and your focus is on the works of art for which the building was designed.

Spiral staircases, while not very practical as primary steps because they tend to be a hazard, do make the best use of the geometry of space because they require the minimum square footage.

Spirals have also been used universally for such decoration and detailing of sacred construction as on the capitals of Ionic/Greek columns.

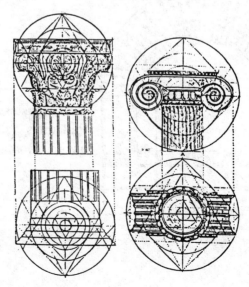

Circles:

One of the best examples of functional sacred design is in the Greek Theater. The design was a physical representation of the goals served by the Greek dramas. *Life plays* dealt with values dramatized by the collective experience of man, nature, and the gods. The theater design followed principles that governed Greek life and its connection to all natural and cosmic experience.

The Greeks, in geometric architectural terms, appreciated the symbolic perfection of the timeless circle in keeping with the unification of the natural laws. Vitruvius' original theater in the round was a masterful study of symmetry and mathematics that integrated many sacred shapes. As already seen, most sacred shapes used in design cannot be limited to one shape.

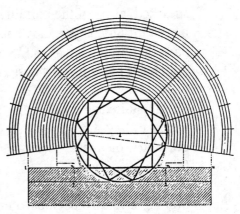

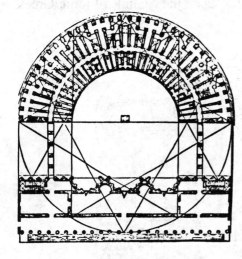

That mastery is also seen in Palladio's reconstruction of the ancient Roman Theater.

Notice the mastery again in the Greek and Roman elevations.

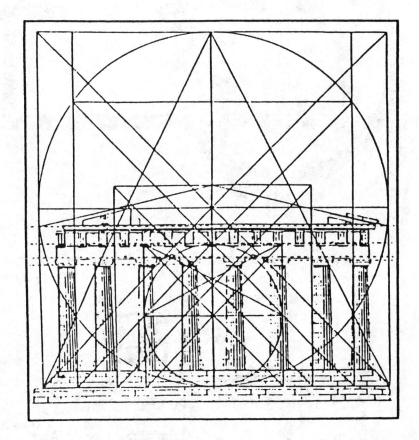

St. Sepulchre's Church, built in the 1100s in Cambridge, England, not only has circles within circles, triangles, and crosses, but includes the cardinal directions and the Bagua. Do you see sacred mandalas in the floor plan?

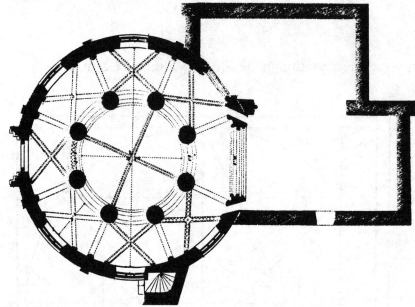

The Cross:

Crosses have been used as universal archetypes by most cultures that include the ankh or the Egyptian symbol of life, Delphic Cross, the upright cross of Jerusalem, and the Byzantine Cross.

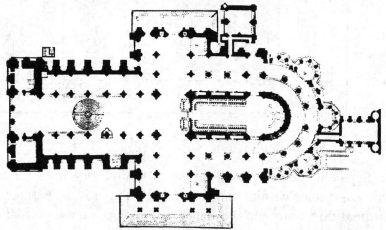

Any church of Romanesque or Gothic design has been constructed in the Latin or elongated cross. It is typical of these churches to have a dome placed at the crossroads apex, confirming the cross with the unity of the sacred circle.

Connections to the Heavens

The ancients knew that the earth was an integral part of the cosmos. Mythologically, the heavens were where the gods lived. When the people respected the heavens and the earth, the gods would take care of their children.

The ancient Greeks built temples for the most honored gods, represented by their earthly locations. Typically, the best sites were at the highest elevation with natural protection, such as the Temple of Athena atop the Acropolis in Athens. This site was chosen so the gods could be as close as possible to the heavens.

The geographical location of sacred sites was also selected by their alignment with the stars, the planets, and with the precision of the equinoxes. Stonehenge, one of the great stone mandalas,[10] was constructed approximately 2000 BC, in Wiltshire, England.

Sonehenge is in celestial alignment with the sun, moon, the Pole Star (which was Polaris at the time of construction), and Sirus. On certain days, such as the Summer Solstice, as seen in the sketch, from the reconstruction of the angle of the sun in 1680 BC,[11] the direct line of light passes through the stone marker and illuminates the altar in the middle of the circle.

---

[10] In the floor plan, there are many mathematical relationships, including squaring the circle, between the sacred shapes and earth geometry. Do you see the interconnecting triangles of the Seal of Solomon?

[11] The earth's polar axis is on an angle that is not parallel to the equator. As the earth rotates, creating day and night as it revolves around the sun, the inclination of the axis does not allow the earth to spin like a top. The *wobble* changes the position of the celestial bodies from the earth's perspective. This effect is called the *shift in the polar axis*, which alters the alignment of sacred structures with the heavens. Because of the shift, the earthly perspective of the alignment has changed from the original construction date.

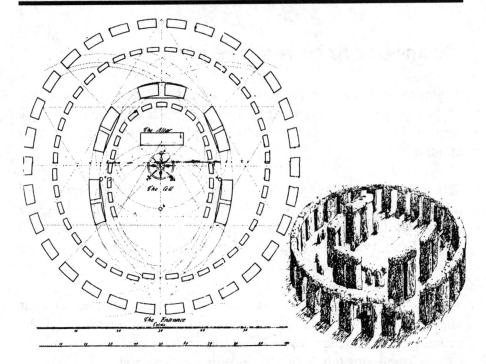

At the great Mayan ruin, Chichen Itza, on the Yucatan Peninsula in Mexico, there are many examples of sacred design. Included in the connection to the heavens is the Mayan worship of the Sun God.[12] Another example of how the ancients married the science of the cosmos with design is again witnessed during the Summer Solstice.

On the bottom stair at the base of the main pyramid, there is a carved serpent's head, which represents time and solar energy. When the sun peaks at the equinox, a serpentine-shaped tail is created by the light and shadow as it falls on the steps. The tail of light extends from the base of the pyramid to the top and into the sacrificial chamber.

As clearly seen in the examples at the Great Pyramid at Giza and the Temple at Luxor, the Egyptians considered cosmic relationships. Due to the mathematical relationship of the latitude of the Great Pyramid, the descending passage was illuminated by Alpha Draconis, which was the pole star of the time.

---

[12] Not unlike the other ancients that believed in the Sun God, isn't it amazing how they understood the sacred or scientific connection that the sun is the sustainer of all life?

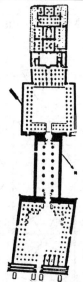

The magnificence of Luxor is a complete expression of Egyptian knowledge, combining science, mathematics, proportions of Phi, geometry, astronomy, and sacred symbolism. Notice, on the floor plan, how the ancient architects aligned the structure with the heavens as they considered the polar axis shift over several hundred years of construction.

Sacred structures were used as ceremonial centers and as symbols that integrated spirit and science; they were also planetary observatories, accurate calendars, and calculators. Additionally, these sacred buildings were said to be vessels to store and transmit powerful earth energies because they are *coincidentally* located at earth magnetic centers.[13]

Beyond location, there is a spiritual connection between the mythology of heavens and earth that appears in sacred design.[14]

Rose window mandalas usually have twelve panes of glass that circle a central one. Often, the center pane depicts Christ surrounded by the *twelve zodiac signs.* Look at the many repetitions of spiral progression in the rose windows of such Gothic churches as Chartres Cathedral and Notre-Dame.

---

[13] Earth magnetics will be explored further in *Natural Science*, Chapter 3.

[14] The astrological representations of the gods ruled certain places on earth. Poseidon (known by the Greeks) or Neptune (the Roman equivalent) was the god of the Sea. Neptune is also the name of one of the outer planets, and in Western Astrology, Neptune rules Pisces, the sign of the fish.

The north and south windows, drawn by A.T. Mann,[o] illustrate two different Golden Mean geometrical relationships.

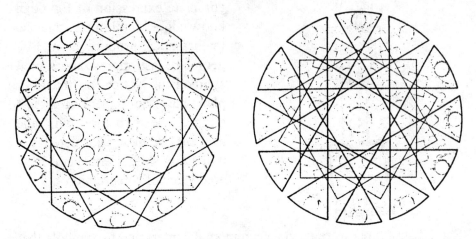

Start to experience structures like an Earth Designer. Notice their relationships to natural laws and archetypal symbolism. The greater your awareness, the more your intuition will augment your own design process.

Exercise: *In your mind's eye, review the architectural design of any gift of antiquity. What does it look like in plan, in elevation, and in three-dimension? Is it in architectural and natural balance? See the structures the way the architects designed them. What are the sacred shapes?*

What are the people doing? What is the mythology? What is the spiritual connection? How do you feel as you experience it?

Do you see any missing dimensions in the original structure that are not in balance? If there are missing dimensions, what was the intention of the architect? What was the feature element that was purposely designed to fill the imbalance?

When you travel, look for the sacredness of form that exists. Look for archetypes in overall site layouts, such as in Saint Peter's square (which happens to be round), or in the cross shape in most historic cathedrals. Look up at the

*domes in churches in the Vatican or in the United States
Capital building.*

*Do you see the life circle mandalas? Look for inlays in
the floor. Look at the woodwork, detailing, and art. Do
they include geometry or sacred symbolism? What do you
see in the designs of today?*

Contemporary Geomancers

For a foundation of Earth Design, it is important to understand that
geomancy is not an ancient phenomenon. There are contemporary
geomancers that are well respected architects. They listen to the
humanitarian call of the natural forces, which gives them insight into the
spiritual and scientific realms, which they then apply to design.

Rudolf Steiner (1861-1925)

Steiner was an Austrian architect that applied *spiritual science*, philosophy, and artistry to his buildings. He felt the role of a designer was to
design a unique form that defines each building's function while
sustaining the activity that takes place within it.

"He believed that the form-creating principles of the earth are derived
from the *Spirits of Form,* beings of a spiritual hierarchy who are involved
in the evolution of the universe and of humanity."[p] The Spirit of Form in
question is the energetic of the natural laws.

Steiner's design suggested that activities were not limited to tasks alone
but to the means by which the inner spirit connected to carry them out.
He felt that designers have a humanitarian responsibility to participate in
and to spiritually enhance the live environment rather than to restrict it.

Steiner used theories on organic growth and materials based upon plants
and animals. He used ideas of movement and harmonic balance and
blended the architecture into the landscape. He based the entirety of his

life's work on the philosophy that human development and science reflected natural patterns.

Frank Lloyd Wright (1867-1959)

"Wright's innovations provided a new direction for freedom and logic in architectural design, and all emphasized the importance of an overall sense of unity and harmony. He stressed the joy of understanding nature, which produces the forms of plants, each responsive to the needs of its environment, each with its basic 'engineering' structure, its material and color, its form and function evolving in its life pattern."[q]

Because of his philosophy, he created environments[15] that were harmonious for modern lifestyles. With his curiosity regarding nature and its structural form, he designed spaces that provided an innate sense of comfort. He created spiritual architecture because his interior/exterior design relationships fully integrated structure with nature.

Discourses on Architecture,[r] written by his associate Viollet-le Duc, suggests that Wright was a student of Pythagoras and Plato and that he understood sacred shapes and symbolism.

> "There is a tight correlation between architectural proportion and the geometry of the granite rhomboids that structured the crust of the earth."

> "One issued out of the order, and both were extensions of the framework underlying the universal order. Since each rhomboid was formed by interlocking pyramids, each defined in turn by four equilateral triangles, nature's wisdom was made apparent in her choice of this most stable of shapes to prevent the internal energy of planets from bursting out. It was to this kind of natural reasoning that architects were to construct sound and stable buildings."

---

[15]   The library in his studio/home was designed in the shape of the sacred Bagua Octagon.

Not unlike Pythagoras' mathematical relationship to tonal sound or the music of the spheres, Wright saw the similarity between music and architecture. "Only the nature of the materials differs. Music and architecture blossom on the same stem; sublimated mathematics. Mathematics as presented by geometry. Geometry is to Architecture only what mathematics is to music." He added the breath of spirit or humanistic qualities to his design.

When Wright was in need of spiritual refreshment and strength, he would spend time in his church of nature. He studied *The Trees of Life*[16] and applied the lessons they taught him to his design. He recognized that trees with deep tap roots would survive violent wind storms, so he designed buildings with deep vertical foundations. He learned that when tree branches cantilevered from the trunk, they would be stable, so he built floors of buildings that would transfer the forces to the vertical core.

In his own words: [s]

> "No part of anything is of great value in itself except as it be an integrate part of the harmonious whole."

> "Form and Function thus become one in design and execution if the nature of the materials and method and purpose are all in unison."

> "Human scale was true building scale."

> "By organic architecture, I mean an architect that develops from within outward harmony with the conditions of its being."

---

[16]   The tree is a universal symbol in ancient mythology that represents the connection between heaven and earth: The Tree of Good and Evil in the Garden of Eden, The *Tree of Life* in the Hebrew Kabbalah, the Scared Oak Groves of the Druids, the Yggdrail world ash tree in the Norse myths, and the Chaldean myths that suggest trees are the center of the world.

> "Man takes a positive hand in creation whenever he puts
> a building on the earth beneath the sun. If he has birth-
> right after all, it must consist in this: that he too, is no less
> a feature of the landscape then the rocks, trees, bears, or
> bees of that nature to which he owes his being."

While Wright's designs reflected his organic philosophy, he used reinforced concrete, which was the modern construction material of the time. Today, as you will learn in Chapter 3, science is discovering that these building materials create toxicities in the environment. If these dangers had been present at the time, I am confident that Wright would have either demanded manufacturers to provide him with suitable building materials or he would have developed them himself.

> "Architecture is that great living creative spirit which
> from generation to generation, from age to age, proceeds,
> persists, creates, according to the nature of man, *and his*
> *circumstance as they changed.*"

Le Corbusier (1887-1965)

As a painter, sculptor, theorist, planner, and architect, Charles Edouard Jeanneret changed the rules and established the tone for contemporary architecture. Le Corbusier, as he had become known, incorporated many levels of meaning in his design, including symbolism and proportion.

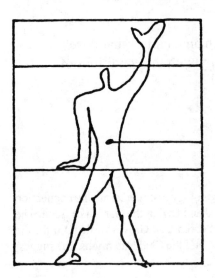

Corbu, as he was affectionately known to students of architecture, used divine proportion and designed a system he called the *Modulor*. This system was a harmonic measurement to the human scale and universally adaptable to architecture. The Modulor was based upon "a six-foot man with his arm upraised, inserted into a square, which was in turn subdivided according to the golden section."[t]

The Modulor became his philosophical emblem and his commitment to discovering an architectural order equivalent to that of natural creation. The Modulor helped to regulate the relationships between elements of different scales that resulted in unique grid patterns in his design. However, if a design did not look right to Corbu's eye, he would make visual modifications, thereby adding the humanitarian factor.

From the poems he wrote about the natural forces: sun, moon, water, and shadow, Corbu incorporated the natural laws in his design. He said, "the landscape which is to be seen must be preserved, not built on in haphazard fashion. A wise plan should provide the resources of nature: architectural forms of great sculptural value must be created. The primitivism of his late works should be received with the ethical perspective of a search for the roots of architecture, an attempt at touching upon the basis of psychic experience, and the old obsession of harmony with nature."[u]

In probably his most famous building, The Chapel of Notre Dame du Hut at Ronchamp, Corbu reflected upon sacred imagery and forms of past and present architecture. The building is a beautiful sculpture that is perfectly integrated into the landscape.

While Corbu was a masterful geometric and organic architect, it is difficult for me to qualify him as a current geomancer because one source validated his involvement with the Third Reich. Geomancers base design on universal laws that include *true* humanitarian principles; however, his work is too important for me to exclude.

We have seen *"geomancy as the art of finding the right place and time for any human activity*. It is an ancient form of sacred, ecological land-use planning. Originally integrating the study of ecology, geology, dowsing, earth acupuncture, architecture, sacred geometry, harmonics or music, dance, seasonal myths and rituals, astronomy, astrology, and cosmology, it can also be viewed as the Mother of the natural sciences."[v]

When geomancy or sacred earth geometry is used, we add its dimension to our environments. We are able to come full circle by including the sacred triangle of Science (mind), Design (body), and Creativity (spirit).

*"You must understand what is at stake.
The truth you are pursuing is as important
as the evolution of the universe itself, for
it enables evolution to continue."* [a]

Natural Science

Because the natural science of geomancy has mystical aspects, our Western minds may need validation that earth energy really exists. The new scientists have discovered geomagnetic relationships that have provided scientific credibility. Many of these scientists have interpreted their findings though their spiritual and humanitarian philosophies, further validating that geomancy is a tool to enhance personal and planetary well-being, with grounded mystical aspects.

Scientists have explained that the earth is circled in channels of bio-magnetic energy. Geomagnetics is the science that deals with the effects of the earth's magnetic and electric forces. Magnetics are integral to the balance of nature, and therefore, important to Earth Design.

Following is a brief examination of current work in the new natural sciences which connect earth Chi to our environment. We will further examine how this connection affects us.

Ancient Science: Earth Acupuncture?

The ancients recognized that the earth is alive with energy forces that pulsate across its surface. By understanding the human circulatory and energy systems, they identified geomantic channels of energy around and through the earth. Sacred structures were located according to earth energy and the ancients' physical, emotional, and spiritual associations toward the landscape.

Did the builders of these structures understand Chi? By divining[1] sacred structures, did they also modify the earth's energies so positive effects would result? Did they practice Earth Design?

Early man recognized this energy through an instinctive ability to feel the energetics of a site. Many researchers theorize that the ancients believed that the circulatory channels created patterns of energy that stimulated both well-being and expanded awareness. They speculated that sacred structures were located in areas of high energy concentrations to maximize their healing benefits.

Consider how megalithic stone structures could be identified as earth acupuncture [2] needles. On a worldwide level, these stones, or any sacred

---

[1] Divining is practicing the tools of divination.

[2] This is a wonderful analogy in many ways. Acupuncture is the Chinese science where the practitioner inserts painless needles into the energetic channels of the body to redirect or modify Chi and maximize healing potential.

The Acupuncturists throughout history recognized how the energy 'meridians affect physical healing, consciousness, and spiritual growth.

Chinese medicine views the body as a unified entity in the same way as we analyze an Earth Design project. Acupuncturists understand that each body part is integral and at the effect of all the others. They find the solution to the cause instead of treating the ailment, thereby eliminating the condition.

We are beginning to break from our limiting western belief systems and experience acupuncture as an effective method of healing. In accordance with the Chinese holistic philosophy, we need to look at ourselves, our immediate environments, and the planet in the same unified way.

structure such as the pyramids, Gothic cathedrals, and stone circles, are all *coincidentally* located on sites of high energetic concentrations. These sites alter or redirect energy flow, thereby producing a significant effect on people and the environment.

> A.T. Mann, in his fascinating book, Sacred Architecture,[b] shares an experience about how earth acupuncture affected a site in Malvern, Worcestershire. At this location, no one could find an explanation for an epidemic of multiple sclerosis.
>
> Mann and ten dowsers[3] felt the problem may have been caused by misdirected earth energy. The group assembled in an area where it was believed that energy meridians crossed. This was the same unlucky land where the property owner had cattle and plant growth problems.
>
> Each dowser felt the energy so strongly that it was difficult to follow the energy line up the hill. At the top, the dowsers experienced energy so scattered and disorganized that it even caused many of them to feel sick.
>
> Conversations with the land owner revealed that there had been a stone circle in that location which was destroyed a few hundred years earlier. The dowsers were confident that the land and the health problems were directly affected by the energy disarray.

---

[3] *Dowsers* are individuals with heightened sensitivity that have a natural ability to determine where water and electromagnetic lines are located.

Dowsing provides answers to how the ancients knew where to locate the sacred sites, and it is regaining popularity. Even Albert Einstein found dowsing fascinating; he believed that some day electromagnetism would hold the answers of the universe.

For more information, contact The American Society of Dowsers, St. Johnsonbury, Vermont.

Observational Discovery

Current rediscovery of planetary energetics began in the 1700s by William Stukeley (1687-1765) and William Blake (1757-1827) at sacred sites in Britain and Europe. These men began to notice that the sites were mysteriously connected. Like children connecting the dots, they saw distinct lines that were systematically arranged.

Stukeley[4] even described the classic site configuration. He saw *dragon and serpent shapes* in the sacred site landscape and said, "These earth giants lay trapped within the hills, mountains and waters of the land, waiting to be discovered and utilized by enlightened humanity."[c] How did Stukeley *coincidentally* know that he was speaking about geomancy in ancient Chinese terms?

Alfred Watkins (1855-1935), an English photographer and inventor, observed that many holy places, such as churches, burial sites and mounds, stone circles, monuments, castles, legendary trees, and cross-roads, were connected by organized lines. He also noticed the English landscape was laid out in a web that linked all the sacred sites.

Ley lines, as Watkins referred to them, often marked and connected up to twelve sites. Stonehenge and Salisbury Cathedral, for example, are only six miles apart.

He noticed the *leys* seemed to follow some kind of pattern, usually terminating with a hill or mountain tops. He suggested, "they were like fairy chains[5] stretching from mountain peak to mountain peak."[d]

Other natural scientists, such as Peter Caddy in Scotland and Joseph Heinsch in Germany, recognized that this phenomenon was not limited to England. Ley lines connected sites throughout the globe.

---

[4]   His name suggests a sacred connection: Stucke-LEY (ley lines).

[5]   The Chinese understood the energetic meridians in the earth before this recent discovery. They referred to them as the paths of the *dragon current* or *dragon lines*.

What are these fields of energy connecting the sacred sites? What is this world-wide mapping system? What is the mysterious secret of the living organism we call Earth?

The ley lines began to be recognized as energetic pathways having a humanitarian influence. The following are excerpts from the article, *The Ley Hunters*,[e] by Richard Leviton:

> "Guy Underwood and T. C. Lethbridge introduced the energetic concept of the leys as pathways carrying an etheric but detectable current of unusual, subtle energy, a mysterious stream of terrestrial magnetism."

This is Chi!

> Their findings further suggest "that these energy lines had been recognized and utilized by ancient humans for positive uses in their landscape temples, themselves situated strategically at points along the ley pathways."

> In the booklet, *Leylines and Ecology*, William Bloom and Marko Pogacnik state, "Ley lines are the essential structures of the etheric body of the Earth Spirit."

Earth energy is the mysterious glue of spirit!

> "The life-enhancing radiation of ley lines is best understood by experiencing them, by feeling them as energy fields that affect the whole electric human being. Such human expressions of consciousness as meditation, prayer, worship, ritual, and ceremony are recommended for ley line centers. Each of these methods involves raising human awareness to reach and draw in new energy fields. Ley centers can enhance human consciousness by revelation because at such places, both dense and etheric matter vibrate at higher, therefore more conscious frequencies."

Due to the frequency of sightings, Tony Web proposed that the grid was linked to *UFO* (unidentified flying objects) navigation routes. While there is no proof, there is interesting observational validation.

> Sedona, Arizona, is a popular tourist area that has an intersection of leys creating high energy concentrations or vortexes. Most residents will volunteer that sightings are a common occurrence. It is speculated that spaceships (if they exist) run on electro and magnetic energy, and the power spots of Sedona are easy-to-access fueling stations.

In all scientific seriousness, the fact remains that modern equipment provides validation that the earth has areas with varying energetic concentrations.

Scientific Research

Beyond the energetics of the leys, the husband and wife team of William Becker and Bethe Hagens developed a planetary grid/mapping system based upon ley locations and sacred sites. Combined with the work of Michael Behrend, they discovered that sites in Britain were mathematically aligned according to multiples of fixed distances that formed geometrical figures.

Exercise: *What do you think they found? Take a few minutes and have some fun. What do you think? The answer is in your subconscious. Ask.*

> *If nothing is coincidental, what does your intuition and understanding of natural law theorize? What do you see?*

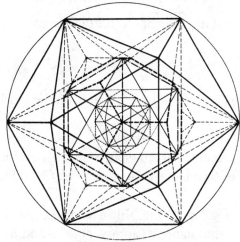

Becker and Hagens *linked the mathematics of the Platonic Solids and Pythagorean geometry*. Did you intuitively figure it out?

When the five Platonic solids are overlaid on top of each other, the solid volumes form a perfect sphere. Then, when the lines of all the volumes are combined, a systematic and uniform web is created.

As represented in the graphic, the connection of the lines form fifteen rings that symmetrically cut the earth sphere into two halves. Becker and Hagens call this mathematical occurrence the *Rings of Gaia.* These rings form sixty-two vortex intersections, and one-hundred-twenty-identical Pythagorean right angle triangles. This special triangle is also known as an MR Triangle.[6]

Earth Design is the connection between sacred geometry (design) and planetary energetics (spirit), synthesized by science.

There are many other universally recognized scientific, mathematical, historical, and mythological *coincidences* that occur on ley lines and at their intersection points. Becker and Hagens outline significant relationships at *each* of the sixty-two MR Triangle intersections.

---

[6] The MR Triangle is also identified as the Meridian Triangle and the United Vector Geometry (UVG) that mathematically segments the earth sphere into the 120 identical triangles.

To name just a few that are relevant to Earth Design:

Location:

MR Triangles connect all sacred sites on the world-wide macro grid.

The triangles connect Greenwich, England, (the location that sets the standard of time), the Vatican, and the Great Pyramid at Giza.

On the micro grids of the Nile Delta, the great pyramids are connected to the ancient Library at Alexandra, King Herod's palace, and the Temple of Solomon.

In one of the European macro triangles, Glastonbury, Stonehenge, and Avebury are connected.

Mathematics:

When eight MR Triangles are connected and structurally joined at their 36-degree apex, they create the exact proportion of The Great Pyramid at Giza and the Golden Mean.

Twenty-eight MR Triangles form a squared circle. Does this sound familiar?

Mythological:

The MR triangle describes Egypt as "*Land of MR.*" *The MR triangular hoe* is referred to throughout Egyptian hieroglyphics; it means *to cultivate,* or *to love.*

MR triangles were said to contain the knowledge of Thoth, the Egyptian god of speech, wisdom, and magic. Thoth is the equivalent of the Greek god Hermes. *As above, So below* is the same concept as Yin-Yang[7] but through Hermetic wisdom.

---

[7] Can Yin-Yang be scientifically explained, "For every action there is an equal and opposite reaction?" I think so!

As we have touched briefly upon the sacred connections of science, geomantic location, design, and spirit, you can begin to appreciate why Becker and Hagens believe that the planetary grid is the living network of Gaia. In their article, *The Rings of Gaia,*[f] Becker and Hagens include a quote from geomancer Pythagoras, whom they define as a "Shaman-geomancer":

> "The experience of life in a finite, limited body is specifically for the purpose of discovering and manifesting supernatural existence within the finite!"

They continue to write, "If, as the MR Triangles suggest, the Earth's body is analogous to a human body, the intersections of the planetary rings may mark planetary chakras. By our ancient attention to these rings, we may have actually imprinted it upon our collective species memory, thus creating enduring geographical patterns of human energy and emotion. Thus, because of its resonance with the molecular carbon and cellular structures that compose our physical bodies, it is predictable that the essence of the rings of Gaia should be powerful within us."[g]

In the paraphrased words of Joseph Campbell and the Native Americans' mythological *Spider Woman*, "Man is merely a strand in the web, but what we do affects the whole web."

We are here to create a blessed life for ourselves and for those with which we share the earth.

We have been provided with the tools!

Buckminster Fuller was a great geomancer, scientist, architect, engineer, mathematician, and inventor who used earth tools in philosophical and spiritual ways. "Bucky" combined artistry, science, and technology as a system for organizing our experience of the universe. His philosophy includes the view that the universe is an organization of generative principles,[8] manifested as energy systems which incorporate into our very being and experience.

By observing nature, Bucky realized that man's first homes were domes of caves and vaulted branches of trees. He also understood that the Platonic Solids were the building blocks of the universe and that nature was mathematically organized. He applied the criss-crossing triangles of the Platonic Solids to artistically, scientifically, and technologically recreate the natural dome form.

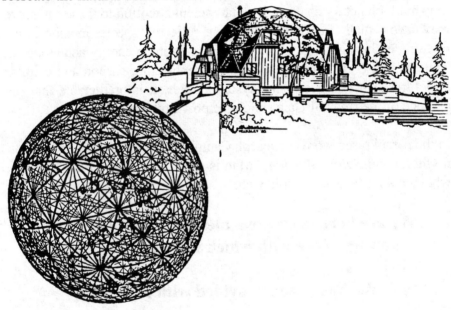

His studies of the earth form are the same as the Rings of Gaia. *Coincidence?* He applied the energetic intellect of the earth and the flowing biomagnetic veins of the Rings of Gaia to create an architectural manifestation. Bucky's genius is best known and appreciated in his design of the geodesic dome.

---

[8]   You will learn how to use the Generative Cycle in Chapter 5, *Feng Shui.*

"These visible geometric natural structures were but manifestations of the invisible, because of the infra-censorial structuring of nature's universal dynamic mathematical cellular agglomerates."[h]

Thinking about the enormous range of the macro and micro modules of the universe, he intuitively realized and stated,

"The Physical and Metaphysical are altogether <u>One</u> Reality."

He even played with the phrase:

*"D-**OM**-e is H-**OM**-e, using the syllable "**OM**"*[9] *or "Domas" (God) and the revelation that man travels though the W-**OM**-b to get to the T-**OM**-b."*

Time Magazine (Jan 10, 1964) not only recognized the geodesic dome as a "unique American contribution to architecture, as a kind of benchmark of the universe, but in the words of the 17th century mystic, Jakob Boehem, it was a Signature of God."[i]

Magnetics

Magnetic earth lines are conduits of energy. Magnetic energy is one direct form of Chi. Through sophisticated equipment, science confirms that energy is in constant movement throughout the earth. Magnetic energy sometimes creates light that we can see in the Aurora Borealis or the Northern Lights, electrical lightning storms, and the bluish white light of Saint Elmo's Fire.

---

[9]   Please refer to *"Om Ma Ni Pad Me Hum,"* in Chapter 5, *Feng Shui.*

As with all Chi, earth magnetics are constantly in flux and influenced by altitude, humidity, temperature, and geographical location. Scientists have recently discovered that there are subatomic magnetic particles in the brain tissue of animals such as pigeons, salmons, sea mammals, and insects. These animals instinctively know how to navigate, using the earth's biomagnetic grid as a guide.

Even plants like the sunflower align their leaves to the north-south magnetic axis. Why shouldn't we align ourselves to the magnetics, just like our animal and plant brothers and sisters? The ancient geomancers observed that planetary movements affected the nature and movement of the earth's magnetic fields. Just like the animals, people would instinctively feel the energy when selecting temple locations. At the time, it was not important to prove the circuits of the subterranean energy grid existed. Dowsers felt the effects through their nervous systems. We too have magnetic particles in our brains. Could this explain why some people instinctively sleep with their head facing magnetic north?

Because of the iron ore composition of the earth and other factors, the electromagnetics of the earth are also affected by magnetic and gravitational pulls of the planets in our solar system. The earth and its relationship to planetary magnetics have a direct influence on the human body, which provides a scientific explanation of how astrological planetary influences affect our lives. This relationship directly supports the use of astrological local space charts in Earth Design. There is direct planetary influence on the magnetics of the environment and on our bodies when they are aligned to magnetic north.

Examples of *astro-influenced* magnetics and their relationship to the human body include:

> The earth's electrical field reaches its maximum between the third quarter and full moon. This condition affects the human body through its oxygen metabolic rate. It also directly affects greater bodily activity, which causes the viscosity index of blood and lymph fluid to decline.

> "Science documents that the Sun produces solar flare activity, appearing as electromagnetic radiation, and it directly interacts with the earth's field. It is as if the sun's field tweaks the system

of the earth and life on it to make it work. In the cardiac system of a human being, there is an electromagnetic cycle which sets off the actual muscle contractile cells of the heart itself. It seems almost like *Father Sun* and *Mother Earth* are interacting, using these complex fields to communicate with each other."[j]

These explanations form the basis of one added dimension of Earth Design; the relationship of environmental and human Chi as they inherently align with the planetary influences of earth magnetics. You will come to understand this correlation and how to make use of this directional energy in the *Feng Shui* and *Astrology* chapters.

James B. Beal's article, *Earth Environmental Fields*, speculates that "electromagnetic earthquake fields' effect can cause visual hallucinations (and *visual symbolic archetypes of geometric shapes*) by electromagnetic inductions into the brain's visual center. These patterns, spirals, squares, triangles, and other geometric shapes are often observed in laboratory conditions."[k]

Not only does science provide solid evidence that human happiness depends on harmony with magnetic fields, but spiritually, the natural law of this perpetual energetic movement is what maintains the harmonic polarity of Yin and Yang. Who says we are not connected to the sacred universal collective though scientifically proven magnetic forces?

In the words of Buckminster Fuller,

> "We used to say that the scientist brought order out of chaos. The scientists are about to discover that all that was chaotic was in our illiterate and bewildered imagination and fearful ignorance. Our knowledge of the universe, at the present, is only measurable in the *dimensional units of energy*, time, and space. These are mostly above or below the narrow dimensions which we are accustomed to detecting by direct sensing and by conscious awareness. New information is gained whenever we examine the patterns of nature with imagination and without bias."[l]

Science validates that electromagnetic fields influence our entire body. Native peoples knew places of high bio-magnetic energy were too special or too intense for long-term human exposure. Chinese geomancers also recognized the bio-magnetic effects on the human body. They avoided sites directly on the dragon lines when possible or developed and tested remedies to adjust the energetics.

Long-term exposure may be harmful, and electromagnetics may even cause cancer, due to exposure from power-lines and such appliances as microwave ovens, televisions, and computers. Therefore, we need to design holistic[10] environments using *Bau-biological* principles.

Bau-biology: The Holistic Home

The new field of Bau-biology is not limited to the effects of electrical and magnetic radiation. It is a study that has the same holistic approach to the design and construction industry as the Chinese have in their medicine and philosophy.

Bau-biologists view our homes and working environments as all-inclusive entities that support all life on the planet, including functional, health, and ecological requirements.

Bau-biology is broken down and defined as: *Bau,* (rhymes with how) which in German translates into *building or structure*; *Bio* means *life, or of living things. Ecology* is biology that deals with the relationships between living organisms and their environment. Therefore, Bau-biology is, "the impact of building environments upon the health of people, and the application to construct healthy homes and work places. Bau-biology is the science of holistic interactions between life and living."

The Institute for Bau-Biology and Ecology makes a clear statement about its global intent:

---

[10]   Holistic philosophy refers to viewing an entity as a unit rather than a combination of its parts.

"The basic purpose is to help people realize that health hazards exist in their homes and workplaces, and that ignorance of these hazards not only has an adverse effect on their health but in a wider sense, on the survival of the planet."

Bau-biology first developed in Germany and has been a strong ecological and holistic design force in Europe over the past two decades. The reason for designing space should be to ensure the health of people. Fortunately, Bau-biological principles are beginning to be applied to holistic design and construction in the United States.

Observation and Logic

There is much work being done to validate the actual effects of harmful building conditions that exist in our modern environments. Perhaps the statistics are irrelevant when considerations are viewed with personal observation and logic.

Generally speaking, the good news is that the human life span is increasing. However, it also appears that cancer deaths are proportionately growing. Was the *"C"* word as widespread in our conversations fifty years ago? Is cancer as prevalent in third-world countries where electricity is not in demand?

Our general lifestyles are very different from what they were in the past and from what they are in less developed countries. How has our high-tech world affected our health? Can we logically speculate that there is a direct causal relationship?

How do you feel after an airplane flight during which you have been breathing recycled, stale air?

You feel the exposure on an airplane in a real way, but it is not as serious as the unfelt, long-term exposure to other harmful conditions. We spend 90% of our time inside. In our office buildings, we do not feel the effects of recycled air because of the greater spatial volume.

Our buildings are constructed with such synthetic materials as plastics, steel, aluminum, chemically-treated wood, toxic paint, and concrete. Our artificial buildings cannot breathe. Consider what happens when toxicity levels of synthetic materials are circulating in the stale air. What happens to a plant when it is exposed to toxic chemicals? It dies. No wonder why the statistics for cancer are distressingly increasing.

There are even more dolphin deaths in captivity than the public is made aware. Dolphins do not do well living in synthetic salt water and tanks of concrete and steel. While they do receive the best care, living under unnatural conditions causes them great stress and premature death.

Was the word *stress* used as a physical human condition fifty years ago? One of its definitions from a physical science perspective is perfect for our purpose. "Stress is internal force interacting between contiguous parts of the body, caused by external forces." (May I substitute... *External Environmental Factors?*)

Why should we place ourselves at risk? Unfortunately, because we do not experience the effects as obviously as we do on a plane, many of us do not even realize that these harmful conditions exist. Science has validated the potentially dangerous situation of long-term exposure. Not only are we creating greater health risks and making ourselves sick, but we are globally damaging the environment.

Do you remember when fluorocarbons were removed from aerosol cans because of the effect of depleting the ozone layer and causing global warming? Combustion and fuels for heating and cooking give off more carbon dioxide than the plants can process, adding to the greenhouse effect. What are all the other out-gasses, pollutants, and toxins doing to the earth or to its occupants?

Have you ever entered a fabric or carpet store and felt your eyes burning? Do you remember how the halls in high school smelled when the biology class was exploring anatomy? You were experiencing the preservative formaldehyde. What did your eyes and nose tell you about toxicity?

There are toxins is in thousands of products, including such building materials as drywall, decorating products such as fabrics and carpeting, bed sheets and clothing, and even in personal products such as cosmetics and deodorants.

There are over 50,000 chemicals in our modern technological world. How does it feel when you accidentally breathe the vapors from household products? Some of these chemicals are known to be carcinogenic. What percentage of them are unhealthy? Which ones? What happens when they are combined? Frightening, isn't it?

Electromagnetic Findings

Bau-biology is a huge field that is just beginning to be explored. It crosses over into many professions, such as architecture, city and urban planning, design, manufacturing of interior and exterior building materials, construction, furniture, lighting, textile manufacturing, and manufacturing of electrical devices.

Electromagnetic radiation produces serious and unnecessary stress on the human body. It is important to understand where it comes from and what can be done to reduce your exposure. When you learn more about how magnetics influence your body and environments, you will have a better understanding of how Feng Shui and Astrological remedies are felt. However, these remedies still do not solve the environmental hazard concerns.

There are two main sources of electro and magnetic fields: inherent and man-made.

The inherent fields encompass the earth. As we saw in the Dowser story, under high concentration there is little we can do other than move or try to modify the energy with Earth Acupuncture in the tradition of the ancients.

Briefly, man-made electro and magnetic fields are generated by high tension lines, low overhead lines, and underground cables, which are nearly impossible to eliminate. However, in our homes and offices we have greater control over reducing both our direct and long-term exposure.

Everything concerning electricity, such as electrical boxes, duplex outlets, and/or any piece of electrical equipment, whether or not the current is flowing, has the potential to emit harmful fields.

When you walk across a synthetic carpet (nylon is a plastic)[11] and get a shock, you are experiencing an electric field.

"If you hear the spark, you are experiencing 2 volts; if you feel the spark, 3 to 4 volts are present; if you see the spark, you are witnessing a discharge of almost 6 volts.'"

Even if your TV and computer are turned off, or you do not have anything plugged into an outlet, an electrical field is still present and may enter your body. There is no substitute for measuring the actual voltage emission with a specialized meter. When a meter is unavailable, the best rule is to keep all electrical devices at least one arm's length away.

Your computer[12] is probably the worst of all because of its emission and long-term exposure! Where is it? Can you move the hard drive on the other side of your desk and get it further away? If your desk is metal, this suggestion won't work well. Metal, including structural reinforcing bars, acts as a channel or conduit for the field.

Where are the surge protector and the electrical duplex outlets? If they can be reached by your feet, direct electrical radiation is being absorbed into your body.

Is your food preparation area in front of your microwave oven? Not only are you eating food cooked with high frequency

---

[11] Plastics are not only a terrible fire hazard, but the off-gassing from plastics (such as PVC) have been known to be a direct cause of birth defects and cancer.

[12] There is a shielding device that may be personally installed into your computer to minimize the exposure.

electromagnetic waves, but your body, especially your head, is being zapped.

When you do take an accurate reading, it is important to have some facts to evaluate the extent of the risk. While all long-term exposure poses dangerous effects, the potential harm is at its worst while you are sleeping. This is because your system is in a regenerative mode instead of a defensive posture.

According to the original Bau-biological studies in Germany, the recommended maximum fields during sleep are:

Electrical exposure is 20 *millivolts* per meter
(1 Volt= 1000 millivolts); magnetic exposure is one *milligauss.*

An electric blanket can generate up to 48 volts (48,000 millivolts) and 10 milligauss throughout the entire night! An alarm clock on the night stand can radiate up to 100 milligauss.

I recommend that you turn the circuit breaker off to disconnect *all* the electrical currents in your bedroom while you are sleeping. It is possible that the wall furthest from the bed may not be on the same circuit and would be appropriate for plugging in the clock.

It is also important to consider what may be next to the head wall of the bedroom. An exterior air-conditioner, a pool pump, or sleeping next to or above the garage (due to electromagnetic emissions from your car) will generate a field that will affect the bedroom as well. Rebars within the structure will channel the electromagnetic radiation to the bedroom. If the rebars are proximate to your body, you will be affected by the radiation, so there still is not a perfect solution to this post-construction situation.

When a structure is originally designed with all Bau-biological principles, a truly holistic environment can be created. Through awareness, desire, and demand, we will get there, one step at a time.

Natural Science of Today
We are the Pioneers

The new natural sciences, necessary for personal and planetary well-being, call for ecological and environmental change. As with any new industry, there are many problems to be solved. There are limited resource materials and few experts. Like the experimental solutions of Frank Lloyd Wright, the Bau-biological pioneers are learning by doing. We must first understand the need and find the best alternatives within what is currently available.

It is important to learn more about non-toxic and holistic environments by reading the available books.[13] It is also important to be patient with yourself. The more you learn, the more you will need to know. Unfortunately at present, the solutions are usually expensive, and the suppliers who do have complete solutions are too few.

While it is essential to do what you can within the limitations of your existing structures and equipment, the best time to incorporate Bau-biological principles is when you are building a new structure. Consider the building materials, how to minimize electromagnetic exposure, and all other Earth Design principles in the planning stages.

What are the toxic materials, and what can be used as healthy substitutes? What can be done to reduce the unnecessary waste of our natural resources? What kind of energy and money-saving solar, conservational, and recycling equipment can be incorporated into the design? What is the balance between your health and safety and doing what is necessary to meet local building codes?

---

[13] Review the valuable information in such excellent books as in the "References" and: *The Natural House Book*, by David Pearson, The Non-Toxic Home, by Debra Lynn Daddo, and *Places of the Soul*, by Christopher Day, or take the Bau-biology Correspondence Course.

Contact: Helmut Ziehe, The Institute of Bau-biology,
P. O. 387, Clearwater, FL 34615

All these considerations may be addressed as a holistic unit. This will help you avoid such problems as having a bedroom with magnetic-field-conducting rebars in a poured concrete floor slab. What has happened to the richness of wood homes where the structural integrity was as sound as concrete? Doesn't wood feel much better?

There are perfect solutions!

I was watching *"Beyond 2000"* on the *Discovery Channel*, it was fascinating to learn that there is a company in Spain that is fabricating coffins out of crushed almond shells and non-toxic resins.

Not only are the coffins biodegradable and non-polluting, they do not give off toxic fumes during cremation or fabrication. They are less expensive to the consumer. And they are solving major waste problems for the almond industry while preserving our forests. The coffins can be beautifully finished to look like any wood grain, metal, or even granite.

Why isn't this technology being used more often for fine-finished furniture or rough building materials?

This example illustrates how a problem was turned into a profitable and environmentally healthy solution. Everybody wins: the waste problem is solved, the vendor makes money the holistic way, freight carriers use less energy, and all cost savings are passed on to the consumer.

What other natural by-products are causing waste and disposal problems?

Our education and action should require building manufacturers to research products that are more suitable for healthy human usage. It is our responsibility to make building material manufacturers accountable by demanding that materials are personally and globally beneficial. By being respectful of our limited natural resources, they will have to reduce, reuse, and recycle while producing healthy, high-quality building materials.

In our lifetime, we will probably not realize all the dangerous ramifications of our present building materials and construction. However, there are enough obvious consequences for me to logically suggest that it would be more productive to concentrate our efforts on solutions rather than spending time on validating the hazards.

The new natural sciences provide the same powerful applications to our personal environments as do all Earth Design principles. When the conditions in our environments are balanced according to the natural laws and designed with healthy materials, we are aligned with the integrity of the earth spirit.

Natural and Earth Designed structures are "ingrained in the biology and geometry of our bodies. As we begin to connect with the places of spirit in our environment and build structures that will provide lessened health risk, we also begin to connect with places of spirit in our bodies."[n]

Part Two

STRUCTURE and SYSTEMS
The Methods

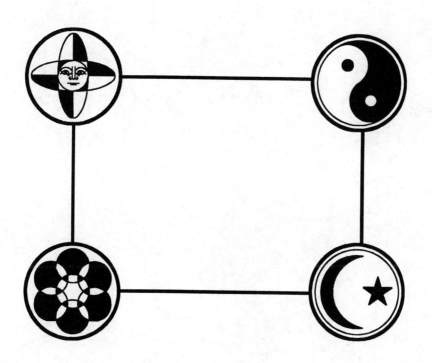

"Walls, windows form the house, the emptiness, which surrounds it gives it its destination. We need beingness, not beingness gives beingness its designation."

Lao Tzu

Intuition

I am sure you realize by now that the principles of Earth Design are not new. They are universal concepts used by geomancers and scientists which connect human life to the spirit of the earth. By studying their applied intuition, creative earth geometry, and historical applications, you can see that design is an integral part of the collective human experience. Ancient architects and natural scientists used all available resources. They solved design problems without limiting their creativity.

Often, we mentally restrict ourselves with the *structures* we put around our minds. Sometimes we forget to apply our intuition, which is what gives us creative vision. Industry leaders use their intuition by taking calculated risks that can gain them a competitive corporate edge. They recognize a need and solve problems by inventing something new.

Intuition is one of the gifts of natural law which we all can use. Intuition to a human being is as powerful as instincts are to animals. Through our intellect, we can discern information that comes through the little voice that exists within each of us.

It can advise us on such simple things as knowing who the caller will be even before the telephone rings. It can also give us greater insights and guidance to fulfill our higher life purpose. Like Wright and Fuller, we can apply our intuitive ideas through the universal experience.

What did Frank Lloyd Wright experience when he saw the tree branch that cantilevered off the trunk? Not only did he recognize the laws of natural growth, he intuitively developed a new approach to architectural design.

Like Wright, Buckminster Fuller intuitively generated innovative architectural techniques. He spoke about intuitive ability as a *work smarter, not harder* approach.

> "The great discoveries of general principles by which the mind of mankind has suddenly leaped forward are not entirely due to the laborious piling up of data upon data until a general principle becomes clear, but are sudden flashes of intuition that come as some exceptionally gifted mind that meshes briefly with a *greater intelligence (intuition)* to obtain a revelation of truth, later to be proved by conventional pragmatic experimentation." [a]

Intuition is a function of your mind, and it is similar to the various parts of your body. Your arms are set in motion by the need to pick something up. You swallow water in response to your thirst. Your intuitive ability is set in motion by your desires.

> From personal experience, intuition provides me with answers relative to the *quality* of my questions. When I ask general questions, I get general answers. If I want *specific* answers, I try to formulate *specific* questions. After receiving an answer, sometimes I realize the question was not formulated properly, or it was not specific enough.

The real work is in asking the right questions. When you are ready to know the answer, you are ready to formulate the right question. The answers to the right questions can change your life.

Sometimes I begin to ask, and the answer is in my head even before I finish asking. Questions such as, "Is working with this client going to be a mutually rewarding experience?" are more direct and easily answered. Other times, the question requires time for the answer to materialize. Often, *coincidences* present themselves, leading to more information that guides me to formulate new questions.

The best way to learn is by being aware as you experience *your own story*. Intuitively, you are your own best teacher. Learn from my process as you begin to watch yours.

> *A few years ago I asked, "What can I do to incorporate my love of interior design and passion for sharing metaphysical work with others?"*

> *Within a week or so, almost like magic, I learned about Feng Shui. As I researched and studied, I began to ask more questions. "How does Feng Shui tie into metaphysics and conventional interior design? How does it tie into other spiritual paths?"*

> *"How can Feng Shui be applied to a mainstream market? **What can I call it?"***

The questions are so important because they are the first step in receiving intuitive answers.

> *Intuitively, I decided to call my thoughts on geomancy "Earth Design." It felt user-friendly, combined my interests in earth geometry and interior design. More questions.*

> *"What will my clients think and should I approach them?"*

> *Because of the mystical aspects of Earth Design, my intuition told me that I must bring it down to earth and provide a solid foundation to satisfy any client skepticism. I must also teach them the benefits of having Earth Design incorporated into their environments.*

I learned more about the subject and applied the grounded information. Coincidentally, I learned about the relevance of Earth magnetics to Feng Shui and Astrology, how the ancients applied Earth and Planetary Consciousness to their architecture, and how Earth-friendly products could be incorporated into non-toxic, healthy environments.

*The more I discovered about "Earth Design," the more excited I got about the magic of intuition and how important it is to the life process. Before my research, I had no idea how the name **Earth Design** was so intuitively perfect.*

Pat of the intuitive process is learning to trust the information you receive. Inner trust is sometimes waiting to make a decision until the answer is *clear!* You can make a decision to not make a decision until you *know* the answer. As with my personal earth design process, the answers took a while to gel and synthesize.

"Guided by their intuitions, everyone will know precisely
what to do and when to do it, and this will fit harmoniously with the actions of others." [b]

Be patient; trusting your intuition is believing in your future. Remember the trip to Hana? It is not the getting or being there. It is the process, *your process.*

You cannot live anyone else's life
Or experience anyone else's process.

Sometimes intuition guides you into what you perceive to be wrong while you are in the middle of it. Looking retrospectively at the event, you will often find it moved you to the place it was necessary to be at the time. Often we are guided into something that only the future knows.

We have a whole lifetime to experience the joy and the lessons of the intuitive process. Intuition, as applied to Earth Design, helps you develop a series of questions and answers needed to help make good decisions. If you make this decision, how will it *holistically* affect everything else?

Take your time to use your intuition.
There is no rush.

With the invention of high-speed equipment in our techno-world, we are often caught in a rat-race pace. We forget to slow down long enough to receive intuitive information or to even ask questions.

> Sometimes I wish fax machines had never been invented because I allow them to make me less tolerant and patient. *Isn't it ironic that fax machines were designed for receiving (in addition to sending)?*

You and I need to slow down to tune in. When you trust your own intuition, it will benefit **all** aspects of your life, including The Added Dimension of Earth Design.

Dimension

Dimension is a very carefully chosen word. On the physical level, dimension is a measurement of length, width, or height in conventional design. *Dimension lines* are used to scale and proportion design elements properly.

From a design perspective, if the dimensions of a sofa are greater than the dimensions of the space, the sofa is too big. This condition is obviously out of balance and may cause *multi-dimensional* problems.

Dimension also suggests the many layers of experience we human beings are capable of integrating into our lives. We can be successful on many levels as well-rounded, personally-satisfied individuals.

When you use intuition as the final step in your life's decisions, the opportunity to create yourself into a multi-dimensional being is enhanced. Multi-dimensional beings have multi-dimensional life experiences, which is the purpose for being alive in the first place.

The greatest dimension of Earth Design is the one Master Lao Tzu shared with us and I quoted in the opening pages. His words remind us that *dimension has no limitation*. His words give us insight regarding the structure of our homes. Lao Tzu says the open space that surrounds the home is what defines it, not the structure itself. As with our spaces, our minds have unlimited potential when they are unrestricted by our mental structures.

When form is defined by its relationship to the surroundings, our environments define and support the structure of our bodies. Why are we not living in caves to satisfy our basic need for shelter? Throughout the course of history, our unlimited minds have designed more creative and beautiful environments.

Your mind is structured by your body, and accordingly, it is not merely an empty shell. Your mind and body are vessels[1] for containing who you are as a personality. Home is not just the shell that defines your body. It is a vessel that has the capacity to contain naturally-balanced earth energies.

Our Homes and Working Environments are Our Second Most Important Vessels!

Through this connection, our sense of security deepens and ultimately opens spiritual vessels. Our soul's essence has the opportunity to create and manifest whatever is desired. When we augment our homes with proper furnishings, finishes, and accessories, we not only surround ourselves in beauty, but maximize our connection to the natural balanced energies that provide greater health, harmony, and prosperity.

No different from the cycles of natural law, the intuitive dimension of Earth Design has macro and micro levels.

---

[1] Kabbalistic or Jewish mysticism describes our body as the vessel in which spirit or soul essence is poured. This vessel is the *structure* that *houses* our mind and spirit.

On the macro level, your intuition helps you to:

Understand the energetics.

Identify energies in your personal environment.

Apply the practices.

On the micro level, your intuition helps to:

Understand specific energetics.

Apply them in relationship to your personal energy and the other occupants of a space.

Turn a dull design into one that has special aesthetic excitement and dimension.

On the spiritual level, your intuition helps to:

Use the energy for spiritual development, intensifying your ability to use intuition when applying Earth Design principles.

Achieve greater health, wealth and prosperity because you are in harmony within your balanced environment.

Ultimately become a catalyst for someone else's inner growth and development.

The dimension of developed intuition will not only help with your Earth Design decisions, but will keep on widening the path for spiritual development. This process adds the dimension of personal growth.

In the words of our friend Bucky,

> "Every time a man uses his know-how, his experience increases and his intellectual advantage automatically increases. Energy cannot decrease. Know-how can only increase. *Wealth,* which combines with *energy* and *intellect (intuition)* can only increase."[c]

Directly from a Master Geomancer:
Use Earth Design for Greater Abundance!

Catch 69!

The more you develop intuition and spiritual essence, the more it is received on all levels.

> *What about my bittersweet relationship with the fax machine?* The life you and I are living is in the *now,* and fax machines are part of life. Instead of allowing machines to speed up my life, I ask my intuition, *"How can a fax machine teach me a lesson that will serve me in another way?"*

> A fax machine is a vessel for receiving. It just sits there quietly, waiting for information coming from elsewhere. The information is not edited, abridged or censored.

> Shall we not think of ourselves as a *facts* machine, without restriction or limitation, as we wait patiently to receive?

Limitations

Limitations are mental structures that keep us away from new possibilities. They are boundaries set up in our minds, restricting intuition, creativity, and accomplishment in life.

Limitations are the boxes in the mind that convince us we cannot do something. Remember the fable about the fox who could not reach the grapes that were hanging too high in the tree? Without asking his intuition to help him figure out a way to reach them, he decided that the grapes were sour.

Our minds create rationalizations and excuses that restrict us from setting goals. "I don't have the time..., I'm too tired..., I don't know what to do..., I'm bored..., I can't...." One day you'll wake up and wish you had made the time.

Initially, it may seem easier to make excuses than to do the work, but there is no personal satisfaction in excuses. Limitations in life affect how you may respond to emotional and spiritual issues. They are often manifested in a physical way.

If there are limitations in life, there are boundaries in space. When there are mental blocks in our heads, we are not capable of seeing through to remove Chi blockages from our environments.

> Do you sit with your back to the door and make yourself vulnerable to what is behind you? Do you sit there because you do not want to see what is coming and you want to avoid dealing with it head on? In school, did you purposely sit where the teacher couldn't see you? At work, do you slip into obscurity? What are you hiding from? Yourself? Your life?

The boxes that restrict you are old, unproductive patterns. They come from a perpetuating spinning wheel of detrimentally low self esteem. They come from a place in the mind that has convinced you that goals cannot be accomplished anyway, so why bother setting them.

You can choose to discard the boxes. When using intuitive guidance, you can learn to make things happen. So start setting the goals, and begin to accomplish them.

A sense of purpose is the first step in setting goals. Low self esteem must be conquered because it is the limitation that makes you a *victim* on all levels. Victims stand in the corner of a room to keep from being *exposed*.

They keep their eyes closed, thinking that they can avoid unfortunate situations. With your eyes open, you have time to see what is coming and move out of the way or be the first to jump on an exciting opportunity.

The more you allow yourself to spin on the Catch 69! wheel, the more you will develop intuition and be intuitively guided into reaching higher goals. This is how to develop the Chi within you.

Using the current mythology of *Star Wars*, personal Chi is *The Force* that lives within you. As your personal Chi continues to develop, you become more awakened to spirit. Personal Chi is the development of the internal force that expands your potential. It is the energy of will, persistence, and capability.

The stronger your personal Chi, the more you are free of self-generated limitations to create the life you desire. Like the ever-expanding circles of Phi, your life will become richer and more abundant.

Again, on what wheel do you want to ride?

Through intuition, you know that by setting a few small goals and with a little work, the goals will be reached and your self esteem will increase. Through a sense of accomplishment, your newly generated pride will allow you to tackle bigger goals.

The sweetness of life is the intuitive universal knowing that the potential of abundance is unlimited. When stretching beyond what you initially perceive to be a limitation, the rewards are exponential. The more goals you set, the more you get done, and the better you feel about yourself. The higher the expectations, the freer you are from limitations, and the more potential you have for abundance.

Life is so good. You are lucky to live in a time and place where there is unlimited potential.

Make it Happen!

When you set the intent, things happen easier and with greater grace.

> "Today I'm going to write a resume; I'll make copies so I can mail them tomorrow, so next week I can make interview appointments, and so on."

Setting the Intent helps to focus and strengthen your determination. Interestingly, when you set the intent, somehow the energy of the universe helps to manifest your desires. Similar to the way we ask our intuition to guide us through a process, the universal energy combines with personal energy to create what we intended.

> From the efforts of writing the resume, set with purposeful intent, desire, and effort, you will land the job that will ultimately position you to ____;[2] it *will* be created. ***It Has Been Willed and Set***[3] into motion.

Setting the intent is somewhat like prayer. It is your personal strength, blended with true heart and conviction. Setting the intent is both within and beyond yourself.

Throughout history there have been many ways of setting the intent, which are as diversified as the many cultures. All cultures have traditional alchemy or ceremony as part of everyday life. As with the various religions of today, there are specific rituals for specific occasions.

Similar to christening a new ship with champagne, there were ceremonies to set the intent for geomancy purposes. When a site was selected, there

---

[2]　*It is your job*, you fill in the blank to set the intent.

[3]　I know I'm sticking my neck out, but I'm going to tell you about an intent that I have already set in motion.

I will be on *The Oprah Winfrey Show* to share my gift of Earth Design. I have already purchased my outfit! Why Oprah? She has created a *vessel* with which to share spiritual beauty with people.

were dance rituals to cure the land, ask the gods' permission, or request that ancestors bless the site to support the intended purpose.

I am familiar with some ceremonies from the Black Hat Sect of Feng Shui. These transcendental cures are the traditional ways they set the intent.[4] This school is based upon Buddhist tradition, so it may be unfamiliar to your way of experiencing personal spirit.

Ceremony needs to be felt in order to be fully realized. It is hard to feel rituals/ceremony created for someone else's purpose to which you may not relate.

> Intuitively, by doing a personal *set the intent ceremony* that is individual to your *will* and circumstance, you begin the process.

Create your own ceremonies, the same way you ask for intuitive guidance. By unfolding spirit, the ceremonies you create will set the intent for unlimited possibilities.

Setting the Intent for Earth Design

First, set the intent for what you would like to accomplish in determining Earth Design solutions.

Exercise: *Go to the area in your home[5] that is under Earth Design consideration. At a time that you will not be disturbed, quiet your mind. Go into the intuitive place within. Without expectation, ask your mind's eye to give you guidance. ASK FOR IT!*

Something that may be of assistance could come up immediately; pay attention to it. Either in your mind or aloud, say something specifically appropriate such as:

---

[4]   Please see *"Om Ma Ni Pad Me Hum,"* Chapter 5, *Feng Shui.*

[5]   If you are setting the intent for the entire house, do this exercise in the entry and move through the individual spaces.

"I want to create a space that will stimulate my well-being and complete success."

Then be specific. The more precise the questions, the clearer the path to the best decision for the intended result!

You will be amazed that when asking with pure intent, your inner self is delighted to answer. I find that when I clear my mind, experience the conditions around me, and ASK, the answers come quickly. Try it! If it helps to light candles, burn some sage, say a traditional or personal prayer, work with a crystal, talisman, or meaningful object, then do so.

Ask again, *"what is it that I really want to accomplish?"*

"What can I do in my house to expand my perception of myself spiritually, emotionally, and physically to remove blocks or limitations?"

Using the information assimilated from observing the laws of nature, and intuition, the energy in your house will tell you what to do. *Be with it*, and give it some time to tell you. Be receptive and aware of the information you receive.

Help!

A couple that was planning to move in the next several years asked me to help them modify the energies in their home to support their plans. I walked inside and used the techniques I have described to you, but nothing came to me. I was stuck!

I began to notice that every inch of horizontal surface, even the chairs and sofas, in the house was full of things. There were piles on top of piles, dead plants, and empty boxes, and more stuff.

I was still stuck! After buying some time with less important design issues, my intuition finally saw through the clutter.

I realized I was being affected by the environmental conditions. I had been stuck because the cluttered vessel (the home) didn't leave any room for me to receive. The clients were also stuck; they were not going anywhere. The mess was holding them back.

Their first project was to clean house, make files for the important papers, put the coffee mugs back in the cabinet, and throw out the things they didn't need. Subsequently, just by clearing off the surfaces, they were able see more clearly and to organize themselves.

Sometimes there is something in your environment that causes a blockage. Ask for guidance again. What does your intuition tell you to ask now? "What is causing me to be stuck?" Take your time, and be patient with yourself.

If the answers do not come right away, set the intent. *"I would like to remove my personal blocks and allow myself to decide what I need in my Earth Design project."* Do not dwell upon the problem; trust that your intuition will provide the answer. Then, let it go and do something enjoyable. When you least expect it, the answer will hit you. Because of your trust, *it will be very clear.*

Once you have the answers, the goal now is to focus and physically put the answers into production. You will also need to create a personal ceremony to make the physical adjustment to further solidify the intended purpose.

As you begin painting:

"Now that I am starting to paint this wall _____ (color), my purpose is to create _____, and through my personal energy of painting, I set into motion _____."

Upon completion:

> *"The energy to accomplish _____ has been set; I will _____ to be created."*

> *"As I move this furniture . . ., as I hang this mirror . . ., as I plant this tree . . . "*

Then, as you let it go, enjoy the beauty of your Earth Design project. Be proud of your efforts. You still have to take action by moving forward toward the desired results.

> The chances of getting that special job will only be created when you expose yourself to the opportunity. How will a prospective employer know what you can do for his company unless you tell him? *"How will Oprah learn about Earth Design if I do not send her a book?"*

It is important to remember NOT to wish for the results of your intent through a predetermined scenario. It does not work that way. As the intent blends with the universe, it will probably turn out differently than your preconception anyway. By prejudging a situation, you limit the grandeur of the possibilities. Letting go of limitations allows opportunities to present themselves as perfect solutions, bringing you closer to your destiny.

> "Intuition is the avenue that you are now being guided to cultivate to bring about a marriage of consciousness. It is the marriage of the male aspect, which is logical, with the female aspect, which is feeling. It involves bringing them together to become one. You need to be able to see, to understand what you are seeing, and to translate the grander vision." [d]

When you look at the cure and fulfillment of the intent in retrospect, you will find that you got exactly what you asked for.[6] It is the way of natural law.

The beauty of Earth Design lies in the process of teaching ourselves higher skills. When these skills, such as trusted intuition, are developed, we fine tune our physical environment and our life through personal power. We arrive at a place of inner truth, which can never be taken away from us.

Common Sense

Common sense is realizing the importance of not discounting the obvious.

> *There was a couple who wanted to start a family. Every day, they had to walk by an antique baby buggy that still had signs of having been in a fire. The subconscious negative energy of the buggy may have hindered the couple from starting a family.*

Let go of the things that do not serve you, such as limiting thoughts and belongings. An old lover may have given you a stuffed animal. Do you need to get on with your life? Get rid of that old thing. Keeping what doesn't serve you holds you back. Be logical; surround yourself with things and people that give back rather than take away.

Be observant; look around.

Perceive the world as if you were still a child.

---

[6]   Be sure about your intent; it is very powerful. As the devil said in the movie *Legends,* "The dreams of youth are the regrets of maturity." Be careful!

Use your five senses to detect negative energy:

Smell: Are there any odors? Is the air musty or stagnant?

Sight: Is there enough light? Is the area worn down or full of trash? Has the plant life been allowed to become overgrown?

Sound: Is anything disturbing you? Are there street noises, squeaky floor boards, or noises from the attic?

Touch: Do you have any intuitive feelings? Does a handrail seem loose and make you feel insecure?

Ask yourself . . . **do you want to *Play* in the space?** Your common sense and intuition will let you know.

Getting Started: The Physical Requirements

1.   A *to scale* floor and site plan.

If you do not have these plans, you can either draw them yourself[7] or get one from your local building department, architect, developer, or surveyor. If you live in a development, the plans used in their promotional materials are usually not accurate; request a copy of the architectural plan.

2.   An architect's scale.

A scale, similar to a ruler, is segmented into units that help you determine the appropriate size of furniture and how much carpet or wallcovering you need. This necessary tool will save you time because it is scaled the same way a floor plan is drawn.

These scales are available at architectural or art supply stores and are well worth the few dollars! Give a sales person five minutes, and I'm sure he/she will show you how to read it.

3.   A tape measure

Before making any purchase, **always** confirm the measurements and actual site conditions. Floor plans are not always accurate!

4.   Tracing paper

Use this paper for energetic overlays and layout schematics.

5.   An natal astrological birth and local space chart.[8]

---

[7]   This is not easy. Get a lesson at the store where you bought the scale. Perhaps a design or architectural student at the store will do it for you.

[8]   If one is not available, you can use the order form at the end of this book.

"The home is the sacred place where you can communicate with the four elements of the universe: earth, water, air, and fire. You mix it with your love and emotions to create magic."

Laura Esquivel

Feng Shui

Traditional Feng Shui

Traditional Feng Shui is 4,000-year-old Chinese geomancy. Feng Shui, like other geomancy, was developed through observing the natural laws and cycles. Because of differences in the humanistic factor and personal intuition, various Feng Shui schools have evolved.

The *Intuitive* or *Form School* assesses shape, form, spatial relationships and environmental conditions such as good soil or the presence of plants and animals. One basic tenet of this school is to surround a site with gentle mountains and have water on one side for natural protection, like Delphi.

The *Black Hat Sect* is similar to practical interior design; however, as with all the schools, logic and intuition are major factors. There are also *mystical cures* handed down through the generations through Black Hat masters. These cures are for *setting the intent* and activating universal energy.

The *Compass School* evaluates Feng Shui principles through directional orientation. Due to earth magnetics, the energies of the cardinal: North, East, South, and West, and the non-cardinal: Northeast, Northwest, Southwest, and Southeast, are different. Similar to Native American teachings, this school uses the *power or medicine* of the eight directions.

These schools are the basis of our study. Because we live in a multi-dimensional and exponential time of growth, Feng Shui as Earth Design is interpreted through the filter of contemporary lifestyle needs. Our interpretation is no different from any other geomancers who, through intuition, incorporated the way they lived through the economic, political, social, and spiritual attitudes of their time.

Energy

Feng Shui is the evaluation of energy, its effects, and how it may be directed. Similar to the relationship of a *flow diagram*, when we visualize energy as an invisible wave moving through space, we will start to experience how and where it exists. The easiest energies to recognize are the ones that we can see, such as water, wind, and sun, or motor vehicle traffic, because we experience these on a physical level.

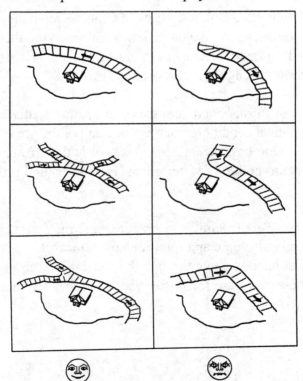

Flowing water is traditionally representative of wealth. When water is flowing at a gentle speed toward your home, it is said to bring financial abundance. When water is flowing away from your home, or if it is flowing too fast, money will come but it may be washed away.

One of the best ways to identify beneficial water flow and direction is to visualize it gently caressing the structure. The more your home appears to be *wrapped in the arms of the water*, the greater the financial potential.

To maximize the benefits of water, you can bring the energy into your house. *It's all done with mirrors.* Hang a mirror on the opposite wall that faces the water. Even if you cannot see the reflection of the water, the beneficial unseen energies will still flow through the room.

If water is running away from your house, use a mirror to symbolically change the direction of the flow. If you hang a mirror so the water reflection appears to move toward you, the negative effects will be reversed.

Consider good interior design; the mirror needs to be in *proportion* to the size of the wall, art work, and furnishings. The *style* of the mirror also needs to be in harmony with the complete design.

The existence of water on your property doesn't need to be natural. You can create a wealthy water environment by adding a fountain, swimming pool, or pond. Water sources must be kept clean and moving. Stagnation of any kind destroys Chi.

If you build a pond, what does your intuition say about the benefit of having fish? Healthy fish are good Chi and represent good luck. How about some red ones for wealth and black ones for a successful career? Before you go dig a big hole in your backyard, wait until we discuss *balance* and *proportion.* Earth Design is a synthesis of many ideas that need to be analyzed together for complete, harmonious solutions.

You have already observed the negative energy of vehicular traffic. Cul-de-sacs and dead-end streets present vehicular and Chi stagnation problems. The energy flows in, but it has no place to go. The solution is to add features that slow or create movement.

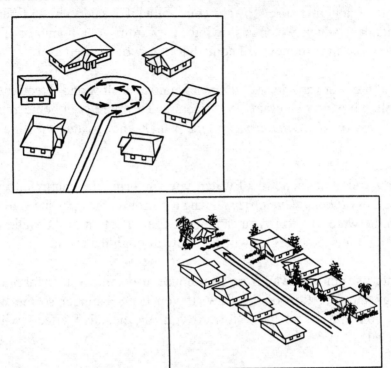

Here are some suggestions: Plant trees that move in the wind, hang bird feeders to entice birds that will circulate the air, put up a weather vane, use a wind chime to create wind music, or add a fountain. Try to soften the space as suggested in the dead-end-street illustration on the right.

Your driveway connects the Chi of the street to your home. It is necessary to disperse the ill effects of car traffic with your driveway. When possible, design your driveway to protect the house from the negative energy. As with all roads or pedestrian paths, Chi most easily flows in soft curves similar to the water in a wide, meandering stream.

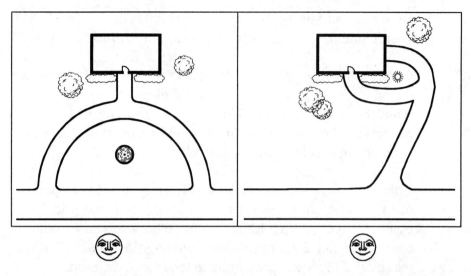

Notice how the balanced site feels. For greater benefit and aesthetic harmony, add a fountain to bring wealth, a light for security and balance, or landscaping for the many benefits of plants.

As with a driveway, have wide walkways in proportion to the landscaping. They should taper outward to the street, thereby inviting Chi and guests to come in. A path that is too narrow or that tapers inward will obstruct and squeeze Chi, limiting financial and career opportunities.

> For example, give the illusion of a wider space or Chi pathway through the selection and installation of appropriate materials. Instead of installing bricks lengthwise in the same direction as the walkway, install the bricks across the path to widen it. This is a great trick.

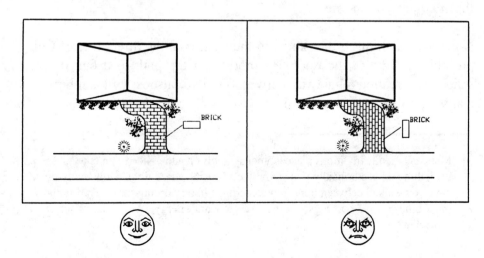

How else can you apply the same principles of this trick? Ask your intuition. What can you do to change the illusion of space?

Consider installing ceramic tile on a 45-degree angle to open up the area. There is more waste with a diagonal installation, so remember to order more. With so many exciting textures and patterns available in various finishes, why focus on the shape that typically installs in a grid formation?

Unless there is some reason to use the grout joints as an accent, use the same color grout as the tile to reduce the grid look, especially when using 12 x 12 tiles. Who wants to be able to count the square feet of a room by counting floor tiles? Consider the scale of the tile in proportion to the size of the room.

Chi flows in undulating waves from the direction of its source rather than in straight or angular lines. When you evaluate a site, a path, or the interior of a space, visualize the tranquil movement of the Chi waves. Use your instincts to determine the effects.

Does the layout benefit Chi flow? Doesn't the gentle flow of Chi from water or air feel beneficial? Doesn't car traffic feel uncomfortable? What can be done to smooth the flow, without compressing it or making it move too fast?

The entry of the structure should be spacious and inviting. Guests will feel welcome because of the presence and affluence of Chi.[1] Do not place an object directly in front of the door as it will block Chi from entering the *mouth* of your home.

Note how the light in the sketch to the right is in the direct line of Chi, prohibiting flow to the door. By modifying the path to a curvilinear shape and creating a gateway between the two bushes, you can beneficially alter the direction of Chi.

---

[1]   Many geomantic traditions place animal symbols on either side of an entry. As you walk through, symbolically you are protected by the guard dogs. How many times have you walked between lions upon entering a library or museum? Traditionally, the Chinese use Foo Dogs; Latins like elephant energy. What makes you feel protected?

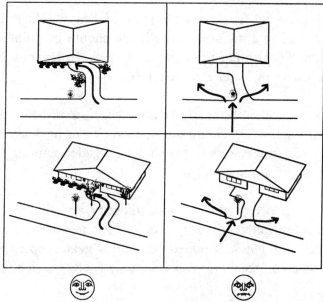

Exercise: *Walk around your home or office. Notice how the ener-*
getics of water, vehicular and pedestrian traffic, and the
path of the sun affect the environment. In your mind's
eye, visualize a flow diagram. See the invisible flow
showing the direction of Chi. Is it fluid and curvilinear?
Is it moving too fast or does it need to be slowed down?
Is something blocking the flow? Can you move the
obstruction or modify the direction of the energy? Is the
energy forced to change direction by a hard angle?

What can you do to soften it? Study the invisible flow
diagram. What does your intuition suggest modifying?
Ask yourself, what are the possible solutions?

Chi and Color

The darks and lights of color are the physical manifestations of sun
energy. How do you feel on a grey winter day or on the first crisp day of
spring?

You have already seen an example of how to compensate for the effects
of sun energy when it is too intense. You can also alter intensity with

color. By painting surfaces with a light color, heat will be reflected. For example, a roof in a hot southern climate should be painted white to reduce interior heat build up. It not only feels better, but there is the additional benefit of lower electrical bills.

Conversely, the darker the color, the more heat is absorbed. The room on the northern exposure of a home surrounded by a heavy leaf canopy does not allow warm sun energy to penetrate. Consider painting the room a dark color to warm it up.

Light and dark translate into the value, intensity, and amount of white or black in a color. Inherently a light color becomes dark in value when more pigment or black is added; the color gets deeper, richer, and warmer. The color peach, for example, may become a rich salmon as it deepens.

A room painted in deep tones is obviously much darker. Careful consideration should be taken when you are adding artificial light. While the room will be brighter and warmer, be careful to avoid glare.

Darker walls, however, will give the illusion that the room is smaller. To minimize this perception, the ceiling should be painted a light color; the furniture should have clean design quality and should be properly *scaled*. The window treatments should blend with the walls rather than accentuate the windows, which may chop up the space.

When you are evaluating sun energy, pay attention to the sun's effects at different times of the day and during seasonal changes. A solution to a problem for one month for only two hours a day may create a greater imbalance during the rest of year. I suggest that you prioritize solutions to have the greatest effect for the maximum amount of time.

What should you do with a space that is always in shadow? Fortunately, most architects consider the sun's pattern on a site when buildings are designed. When shadowing does occur, it is best to use these areas for such storage spaces as pantries or closets. In the event the space is needed for another purpose, use as much artificial light as feasible, and paint the walls a light, bright color. Hang a painting that makes you feel good, or consider a poster of a window with a view of nature.

The Elements

Each of the five elements from Chinese Taoist tradition have their individual energetic properties. From this philosophy, the five elements are the building blocks that individually and in combination create everything on earth.[2] The elements are: *Fire, Earth, Metal, Wood,* and *Water.*

For Earth Design purposes, the elements have specific identifying shapes and construction materials:

WOOD

What do trees look like?

Shape: Trees are cylindrical and tall. The Wood element is represented by columns, narrow buildings, and trunk-like hills.

What are trees made of?

Construction Materials: Wood

---

2   This should be reminiscent of the five Platonic Solids.

Intuitively, what do trees represent?

Symbolizes: Growth, creation and the nourishment cycles

*What kinds of buildings or environments would benefit
by nourishing energy?*

Suitabilities: Memorial and religious buildings, military and commemorative structures, restaurants and catering establishments, nurseries, hospitals, homes, artist studios, dining rooms, children's rooms, and bedrooms in general

FIRE

What do fire flames look like?

Shape: Flames suggest pointed and angular shapes. The Fire element is represented by sharp-peaked mountains, steeply-pointed roofs, and church steeples.

What is fire? What color comes to mind?

Construction Materials:

    Heat: Man-made materials created through heat or chemical processing

    Red: The color of blood for animal products and materials

How does fire feel? Hot and full of movement?

Symbolizes: Action, motivation and intellect

*What kinds of building or environments would benefit by
intellectual energy?*

Suitabilities: Churches (pointed roofs),[3] premises with sloping roofs
that may be domestic, civil or industrial, libraries,
schools, industries using chemical processes, a fire place
and the kitchen stove

EARTH

*On ground level, the earth appears to be _____. (Hint, until
Christopher Columbus many thought the world was _____.)*

Shape: Flat. The Earth element is represented by long, flat hills,
plateaus, table top mountains (mesas), and flat-roofed
buildings.

---

[3]   Traditional Feng Shui practitioners have suggested it may be unwise to live near
a church. They believe that negativity released by church attendees may go to the
next available structure. I suggest that you ask your inner self for your truth.
Perhaps only love is radiating from the church, which would only perpetuate
goodness. If you sense harmful energy, call on your inner strength for protection.

What things are made from earth?

Construction Materials: Clay, bricks and concrete

How does the ground feel?

Symbolizes: Stabile, solid, reliable, and confident

What kinds of building or environments would benefit
by grounded energy?

Suitabilities: Storage areas, stockrooms, garages, industries of tunnel-
ing, farming, construction, engineering and living rooms
(hub of the family)

METAL

What is typically made of metal?
What is the shape?

Shape: Bronze shields and silver coins are round. The Metal
element is gently-rounded hills, buildings with domes,
and round-shaped accessories.

What is the construction material?

Construction Materials: Metal

When you have a lot of "metal"
in your pocket, you feel _____.

Symbolizes: Wealth and financial success

What kinds of buildings or environments would benefit
by abundant energy?

Suitabilities: Monuments, religious and civic buildings, banks, commercial and manufacturing buildings, workshops, jewelry and hardware stores.

WATER

What shape is water?

Shape: Water has no shape and every shape. The Water element suggests irregularity, such as natural topography that has no reason and buildings that have complex curvilinear design.

What materials look like water?

Construction Materials: Glass that is transparent or reflective, mirrors

What is glass representative of?

Symbolizes: Clarity, communication and the transmission of ideas

*What kinds of building or environments would benefit
by mental creativity?*

Suitabilities: Theaters, buildings that print newspapers, advertising agencies, computer development buildings, schools and retail stores.

Exercise: *What elements are represented in your house by its shape and construction materials? Are the shapes and materials in the areas appropriate to the function of the space? What elements are represented by the surrounding structures?*

The elements have a creative/or generative order.[4]

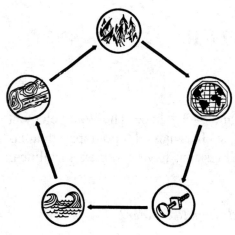

In the creative cycle

Fire produces ash or Earth, Earth creates minerals or Metal, Metal liquefies or condenses into drop-lets (outside a metal cup) producing Water, Water feeds Wood, and Wood creates Fire.

---

[4] Notice how the shape of the cycles are symbolic of the pentagram and the emblem of Pythagoras.

The elements also have a destructive/degenerative order.

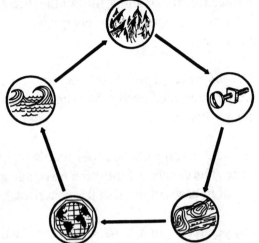

In the destructive cycle [5]

Wood saps Earth energy, Earth blocks Water, Water puts out Fire, Fire melts Metal, and Metal chops Wood.

Through the generative and destructive elemental cycles and their relationship to the surrounding features, favorable or unfavorable conditions may be evaluated. This information should be considered on both micro and macro levels:

The *macro* level refers to the exterior environment. What element(s) is/are represented by the shape/materials of your home and in the neighboring structures? Are the neighboring elements generative or are they destructive?

If they are destructive, use the generative elements in a beautifying and beneficial way. Make modifications to the exterior by adding such decorative features as painting trim in the appropriate generating color. How about red for Fire? Perhaps you can plant foliage with red or burgundy leaves or flowers. How about green for Wood, yellow for Earth, white for Metal, black for Water? Would metal shutters be practical? Add Earth (stone) or Wood details as decorative elements.

---

[5] Consider the other destructive cycles your intuition may reveal: Earth extinguishes Fire, Water covers Earth, and Water rusts Metal.

Block the destructive energy from surrounding buildings or features by using foliage, like in the vehicular traffic example. By adding a reflective surface (mirror or shiny tile) in the direction of the destructive element, you can *bring the negative energy back to the source* and away from your structure.

The *micro* level refers to the intimate environment. What element(s) is/are represented by the shape and materials, furnishings, and accessories in your home.

The house with a pitched roof with wood beams represents a Wood/Fire home. The elements follow the favorable generative cycle, and the energy of that house will nourish the occupants' intellectual creativity.

The occupants in a flat-roofed home with a lot of picture windows are likely to have many disagreements, as the Earth/Water combination follows the unfavorable destructive order. Perhaps there is more to the old cliché, "people in glass (Water) houses shouldn't throw stones (Earth)."

By adding decorative features to your home that represent the generative elements, you can reduce and possibly alleviate the imbalances. By adding a green (Wood) leather (Fire) sofa that has a lot of rounded lines (Metal) to the room with a large amount of glass (Water), Earth will be generated, and the Metal of the curved design will generate Water. Thus, the space and the people will be more harmonious.

Additional solutions may include, but are not limited to, adding a wool area rug (Fire generates Earth), or a wrought iron coffee table, or hanging antique bronze shields (Metal generates Water). You can even put a mirror on the wall opposite the glass window to bring the nourishing energy of the foliage (Wood) into the space.

Did your intuition help you to balance the elements? Keep in mind that an item's form or shape will take precedence over its material. While it is best to reduce the most influential destructive element, I find that when all the elements are represented, there is aesthetic and energetic balance.

It is possible that only one element is represented. Living in South Florida, I see a lot of square, flat-roofed *Earth* homes with ceramic tile on the floors. While this type of construction is affordable and easily maintained, the occupants may feel emotionally stuck into routine.

Go Ahead . . . You Are Alive!

Add some Fire and get motivated:

> Artwork with red as the predominant color
> A wool area rug
> A geometric/angular print fabric

Add some Wood for creativity:

> Floral fabrics or wallcovering
> Furniture with wood details
> A wooden baseboard, wainscot, or molding
> Fresh flowers and plants

Add some Water for mind focus:

> Crystal accessories and vase with fresh flowers
> An indoor running water sculpture
> Sconces with glass shades
> A painting of the ocean

Add Metal for financial growth:

> Bronze door knobs
> A piece of sculpture
> A metal picture frame

Add Earth for stability:

> Terracotta planters
> Natural stepping stone entry
> Ceramic accessories

What else? Be creative and have fun! It is possible that the combination of elements does not fit in the generative or degenerative order. These situations have neutral energies. Decide what you and your family members need more of and feel abundant.

Remember that Earth Design has to do with proportional balance. After balancing the energy, make sure your decorative enhancements are aesthetically balanced as well. Read *Conventional Interior Design*, Chapter 7, to help determine appropriate design qualities such as proportion, scale, elevation, use of texture, harmonious color combinations, functional layout, and maintenance requirements before making purchases.

**Make sure your solutions are in harmony
with the other Earth Design principles.**

Everything is affected by everything else!

Take your time and consider all the recommendations. You will discover that the decisions you make now may be different after you understand the whole Earth Design puzzle.

Exercise: *Are the elements in your home in a generative or destructive order? If they are generative, what are the symbolic benefits? If they are in a destructive sequence, how can you balance the energies while enhancing the beauty? Use the traditional representations as a guide, and intuition for your personal solutions.*

Surrounding Conditions
Exterior Relationships

Balance has been defined as *harmonious cycles represented by the soft characteristics of undulating Chi waves*. The more Chi is able to flow in this manner, the more beneficial a site will be. Consider the difference in the shape of the Appalachian mountains and the Rockies. It is easier for Chi to flow around the soft Appalachians than around the hard angles of the Rockies. This fact is confirmed by the Chi-generating plants and animals, which become scarce after you reach the hard-angled, higher elevations.

Ideal sites like Delphi, which is in the *perfect topographical configuration,* are usually not available or affordable. Perhaps the magic and the sacredness of the ideal sites are best left for everyone to enjoy.

Sedona, Arizona[6] is a magical location sacred to Native American Indians. Many moons ago, the Native Americans recognized Sedona as a place where many different energies converged.

---

6   Sedona is a place where *dragons of good fortune* exist in the landscape. It is located where there are many interconnecting earth magnetic ley lines creating the existence of energy vortexes.

Because of the sacredness of Sedona, the Indians only used the space for food and prayer.[7]

Today, Native Americans still pray in Boynton Canyon, a sacred place of their ancestors where there is a marriage of magnetic (female) and electrical (male) energies, *Yin-Yang.*

A developer saw the beauty of Boynton and thought it would be a wonderful place to build a resort. Disregarding the warnings of the locals, he constructed *Enchantment.* To this day, three different owners have not been able to make it a success. The magic, the ancestors, and the energetics were defiant. The intent of the developer was not in harmony with the *master plan.*

This true story illustrates why Earth Design advocates being in touch with the mystical and spiritual realms. Perhaps one day a developer will *be called* to convert Enchantment into a healing center.

When our urban and rural sites are selected, considerations like those in the story above are not usually an issue. Besides how many of our sites resemble Chinese paintings with the ideal site conditions? More than likely, the sites have not been reserved as sacred places and are energetically approved. We typically select our homes because of their availability, location, economics, and proximity to schools and work.

Balance: Structure to Surroundings

Scale is one of the basic principles of design. If your house is too big or small, it is out of proportion and balance to the rest of the environment. Your home may be at the effect of a neighboring structure.

---

[7] Archaeologists found evidence that the natives lived in the surrounding areas of Sedona but found only ceremonial and hunting tools in Sedona.

The homes in the left sketch are not at the effect of each other. The sketch on the right shows the smaller structure at the energetic effect of the larger one. If a fence in semi-solid double lattice wood is installed, both homes benefit. A Wood fence will generate the pitched Fire roofs, the overbearing energy will be blocked, and Chi will still be able to flow through.

Notice the need to put all of the principles together when developing solutions. Three separate problems have been solved: two energetic conditions as well as aesthetic privacy for both houses.

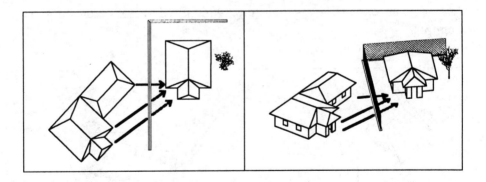

The same conditions may occur with a larger and a smaller mirrored office building. The smaller building would reflect the larger building's dominating energy. An inexpensive solution is to put reflective tinting on the windows of the smaller structure. This measure would also reduce air-conditioning costs. Again, notice how Earth Design solutions are multi-dimensional. Additional solutions are: to plant a hedge or to put reflective material on the roof of the smaller structure. This solution is also appropriate when a residential site is located proximate to a dominant commercial property.

In the sketch with different sized houses, if the fence were not there, there would be another problem. There is a corner of the larger house pointing directly at the smaller house, creating a *secret arrow*. A secret arrow has the same intimidating influence as having a finger pointed at you. Its direct energy splits a space in half, bringing anger, insecurity, destruction, and failure.

The occupants in the house that has the secret arrow will subconsciously feel superior to the occupants in the house receiving its effects. Unless the energy of the secret arrow is blocked, the occupants in the house on the right will feel threatened and unwelcome.

Secret arrows, besides coming from the hard corners of a structure, can also come from a street with a corner directed to the entry. A hedge or fountain will disperse the *Sha* or negative energy while bringing greater energetic benefits. Remember not to block Chi with the solution. Leave the entry as expansive as possible, which will also deter burglary attempts.

The hardest secret arrows to detect are the ones that come from shadows because they are moving relative to the angle of the sun. Shadows are created by such natural or man-made features as a building, tree, or telephone pole. If the shadow cuts the house at significant times of day, it may affect the relationship of the occupants. This is a problem that requires attention. If the shadow cuts across the nursery, where baby takes a nap between 3:00-5:00 p.m., and from the kitchen, where Mom prepares dinner at 4:00, the shadow separates Mom from the baby. Subconsciously, the baby will not receive his needed reassuring and nourishing sleep. The solution is simple: The baby can nap in the family room playpen, which is not affected by the shadow.

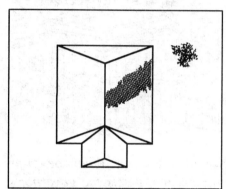

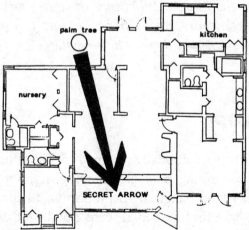

Exercise: In the following sketch, traced from a photo in Smithsonian Magazine, *illustrates a building designed and built without concern for the neighboring structures. Can you pick out the building that did not use Feng Shui principles? What is wrong?*

The Bank of China, in Hong Kong, is inconsistent in scale, according to Howard Chus-Eoan. In the June, 1987, issue of *Time Magazine*, he states, "The acute, pointy ridges would slice through the Yin-Yang, or cosmic balance, thus pricking and angering unwary spirits, who would then direct their anger at buildings toward which the triangles pointed."

The secret arrow is affecting the entire cityscape. *What does your intuition tell you about how the energy affects the governor's mansion in the foreground? Since the governor's personal Chi influences the entire government, what do you think the secret arrow does to the political environment?*

The Landscape

Urban and rural lots are traditionally rectangular. The house and all other features, such as swimming pool, landscaping, lighting, and separate living quarters, must be balanced in proportion to the lot. The best configuration is to have the house in the center of the lot, especially when there are no other major features.

Note the beneficial site, with the front being smaller than the back, which enables Chi to fill the property. If the house is not balanced with the lot, install light fixtures to *bring the back of the property closer* or give the illusion that the back is wider.

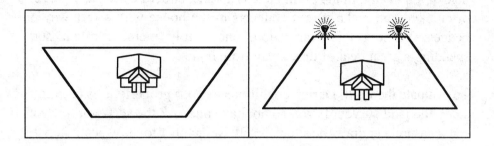

If you cannot see the entire lot because it is on a hill or there are other obstructions, illuminate the unseen areas. By using good Earth Design, if the light is on a solar panel and a sensor, the energy savings and added security will benefit the earth as well as the occupants.

Most Earth Design is common sense. When you can see the entire lot, you have a greater sense of security. When you live in subconscious comfort, you are more at ease, more efficient and successful. Wouldn't the occupants in a building facing uphill feel like life is hard and an upward struggle? Wouldn't it feel better at the top?

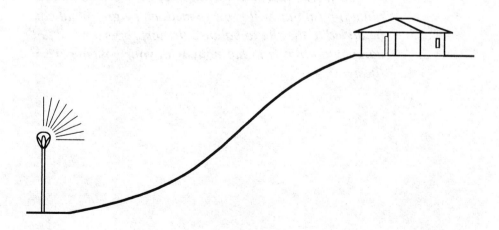

When a structure is not centered on a lot, balance the site with plant material, a fountain or pool, and spot lights. It is the same as filling the hole of Yin-Yang. In the event there is another structure such as a gazebo or chickee hut, make sure it connects to the house with a walkway or hedges. Without this connection, one family member might start spending a great deal of time away from home.

To evaluate the Earth Design conditions of your property, it is easiest to study the land survey. If you do not have one, ask the surveyor,[8] or you can measure and draw the site yourself. Remember to draw accurately to scale and locate the major features.

Exercise: *Look at your site plan. Are all the elements in proportion to each other? What features could be tied together? Are there any other problems on the site? Are there secret arrows coming from the street, neighboring houses, or shadows? Is the sun having a positive effect on the window locations? Are the "elements," both shape and materials, of the surrounding structures in harmony? Are there any other unbalanced energies that are affecting the site?*

Is there a feature on the site that is too big in proportion to everything else? How can it be made smaller? It is easy to trim a tree that is dwarfing the foliage below or to plant a bush that will grow to medium height. What can be added to the site to balance the disproportion? What can you do that is in harmony with your contemporary lifestyle?

---

[8]   By law, sites are surveyed prior to the property being purchased.

A good rule for balance is the asymmetric triangle rule. Instead of building a pyramid, how can you use the ancient sacred shapes? Locate two major features, and fill the missing triangular point with the proper highlight.

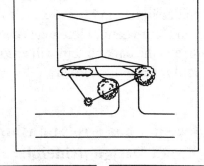

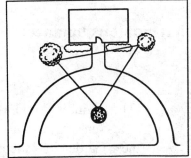 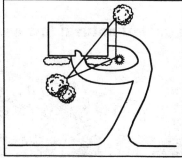

What are some solutions? Use the concepts of all the principles we have already addressed. If your site can accommodate a *wealth generating* swimming pool, use the ideas about natural bodies of water.

How can you design the pool so it:

Fits on the site in proportional relationship?

Has the illusion/feeling of water flowing toward the house? (Perhaps a fountain can be installed at the end furthest from the house as part of the filtering system.)

Appears to *wrap the house in the arms of the water*?

What have you learned about Chi flow? Perhaps the pool should have a natural shape, which is more aesthetically pleasing and avoids the risk of creating a secret arrow. What have you learned about the elements?

Perhaps you can add the Earth element with flat flagstone rocks that are brick color as the edge trim instead of white concrete.

What have you learned about color? Why not paint the inside black, the representational color for the Water element, instead of sky blue? Ask your contractor. Consider finish and texture; will the bottom age to a patina that gets better and more natural looking? Black will solidify your opportunity for wealth, and the dark bottom will absorb more of the sun's energy, making the pool inherently warmer.

Every decision has a relationship to an Earth Design principle.

All is part of natural law and harmonious balance!

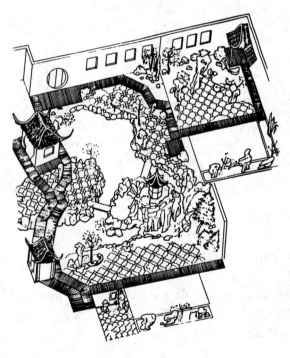

The layout is from Dr. Sun Yat-Sun's Classical Chinese Garden in Vancouver, British Columbia. Traditional Chinese homes were laid out around a central courtyard to *bring the outside in.*[9] This layout enabled all the natural beauty, enhanced by man-made creativity, to become part of the living experience, thus enhancing personal spiritual development.

---

[9] This was one of *Frank Lloyd Wright's* prominent design concepts. He used leaded glass windows and positioned them to maximize natural light. As Chi entered the space, the faceted pieces of glass acted like crystal prisms to disperse Chi throughout the interior volume.

Catch 69! The Chinese understood that by designing our spaces within the harmony of the natural laws and by bringing them inside, we feed our souls. When our souls are well fed, we are more sensitive and make better decisions. The greater our awareness, the greater the potential of fulfilling our dreams. The more that is shared, the more that comes back.

You have the opportunity to make choices to make your home more beautiful and spiritually enhancing without spending a lot of money. If you do not have the area or finances for a pool, perhaps you can purchase an inexpensive bird bath or self circulating fountain. A water pump costs less than a hundred dollars. Do-it-yourself. Home builder stores offer many inexpensive ideas.

When you buy plants, please ask the right questions:

How big/wide do they get, and how long before they reach their mature size?

Do they need full/moderate sun?

How much maintenance is required?

Are they messy when the flowers or leaves drop?

Do the flowers or leaves stain?

Does the plant go through yearly cycles, changing its aesthetic appearance?

Do the plants drink a lot of water?[10]

Will the color and texture of the new plants be aesthetically balanced with the existing ones?

---

[10] By using the water-wise concept of *Xeriscape*, you can design your landscape with water-conserving efficiency.

Home builder stores usually have excellent prices on plants and knowledgeable salespeople. Look at the how-to book section. How can you apply Earth Design?

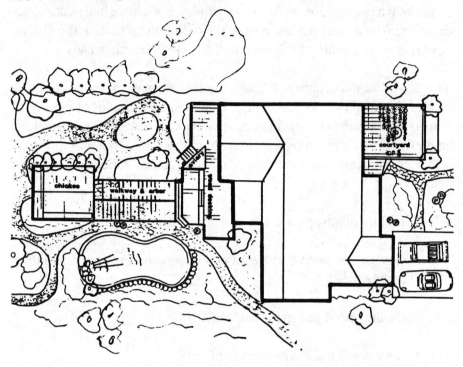

Look how close the house is to the front of the lot. Notice how the site is balanced by using Earth Design:

> The plan shows an integration between the interior and exterior. The exterior is an aesthetic extension of the living space. The entire lot is a balanced entity, with all the features making a *cohesive usable whole*.

> The house, with its pool in the back and fountain in the courtyard, is surrounded by water on both sides. The pool has a natural fountain at the farthest end, so water flows toward the house.

> The courtyard with its red brick tile floor coordinates with the *Earth* of the red barrel roof tile. There is a canopy of purple and red bougainvillea to protect the inside from excessive heat while the flower colors represent wealth.

The existing chickee was connected to the house with a red stamped concrete walkway (Fire/Earth), which is less expensive than tile or stone. The stamped design is an irregular stone in the Water shape, which is sized in proportion to the area. Because of the Fire shape roof of the house and chickee, the orchid arbor was also designed with that shape. The arbor and deck are constructed of Wood, which generates and balances the *Fire* energy.

Water was used in the representational form of the soft curvi-linear lines of the walkways. The curved lines maximize Chi flow and balance the angularity of the house.

All the plants were intended to create visual and acoustic privacy from the neighboring lots and the street. Additionally, intimate seating areas were designed throughout the property from the walk and planted areas. The magical tropical paradise *sanctuary* was just what the occupants needed for personal serenity from their high-pressure professions.

Note the 50-foot high palm trees. If the site had been oriented on an east/west axis, instead of north/south, can you see how the shadow of the palms would have created secret arrows, cutting the house in half?

Pay close attention to the proportion and scale of all the features. View your site as a three-dimensional canvas. Create your Chinese painting with consideration to the volumes, voids, textures, colors, elevation changes and height relationships, materials, and movement. Are they all in balance?

Do you see the conceptual resemblance between the Chinese home and the one that fits in our urban landscape? Can you visualize the movement of energy in an invisible flow diagram?

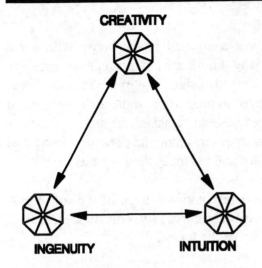

CREATIVITY

INGENUITY   **INTUITION**

It does not matter how big your property is or how much money you choose to invest. All you need to practice Earth Design is intuition combined with creativity and ingenuity.

Interior Relationships

Chi Flow

The most important aspect to consider is the way Chi moves through space. View your home or office as if it was a living organism. Chi flow is analogous to the involuntary function of your heart pumping blood through your body. You don't have to ask it to do the job, the way you voluntarily ask your arm to lift. Your heart just pumps, as Chi just flows. You do have the capacity to monitor and direct Chi to receive its maximum benefits. To review, the main sources of nurturing and regenerating Chi come from the center of the earth, the Sun, and planetary influences.

Looking again at our homes and offices as our most important secondary vessels, we need to bring Chi from the outside through our doors and windows. Doors and windows are the *circulatory system* of our house, and hallways are the veins that direct Chi through the rooms.

The front door, which may or not be the one most frequently used, is the primary source of Chi. The front door is as important to your home as the nose and mouth are to your body. The front door is also important because it symbolizes the transition between your external and internal worlds.

The exterior entry must be open and inviting. A hidden door will not allow vital Chi into the home. Think intuitively; if your front door is not visible or inviting, people will not visit nor will opportunity flow. In the corporate environment, clients may not want to enter.

Exercise: *Think about the different kinds of energies that are coming into your home through the doors and windows. In your mind's eye, draw flow diagrams indicating Chi movement. Visualize the floor plan sketch in three dimension. Are the energies positive?*

Ask yourself how the energy feels in your body. Your body knows when you are vulnerable or safe. It feels at ease or uncomfortable. Learn to feel the effects and the cause.

What kind of energies are there? Are they moving with the light, the air, or the flow of water? Are they natural or man-made? Favorable or unfavorable? Is the Chi moving in harmonious perfection by filling the space and gently flowing out? How does the energy pass through the doors, move through the rooms and around the wall partitions? What can you do to enhance the positive energies moving through your house? What can you do to deter such negative energy as a secret arrow from even entering your home?

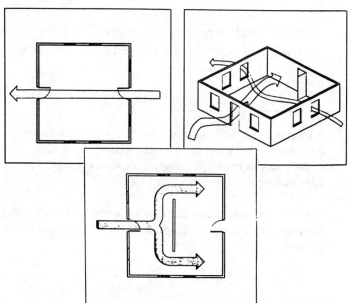

It is possible that Chi may be moving so fast that it blows right through and splits a space in half. When Chi moves too quickly, you can feel the effects by the separated relationships or centralized physical problems.

What do you do? Use your intuition; slow it down. What objects will change the speed, direction, or absorb Chi? In a hotel lobby where there are all sorts of mixed energies and movement, what do you always notice when you walk in? The bouquet of flowers, right.

If it *Catches Your Eye*, it alters Chi.

What objects will make Chi change direction or slow down?

> A wall partition, movable screen, or heavy element will force Chi to move around it.

> A mirror or reflective surface will change the direction of Chi as it bounces off.

> When Chi encounters a crystal ball,[11] water in a fountain, or a fish tank, a hanging mobile or wind chime, the energy will slow down and be diffused in many different directions, similar to the way light moves through a prism.

> An air conditioner or ceiling fan will circulate Chi.

> The sounds from objects, especially from soothing music, will change energy speed and the attitude of the space.

---

[11] A faceted crystal ball can focus energy inward for concentrative work or outward for expansive work. When a crystal is placed over a desk, either effect may occur. Crystals can also push, pull, disperse or scatter energy. Remember to set the intent upon making the physical adjustment.

Use your judgement and intuition to determine the size the crystal needs to be. Remember to consider scale, and don't use a dime-sized crystal for a large picture window.

Musical instruments, like a harp that air circulates through, will not only be a wonderful decorative element but will alter Chi.

Such living objects as plants, animals, and fish are a source of beneficial Chi and will change spatial energetics.

Burning candles and incense change Chi movement and attitude. By watching the flow of the smoke, you will see Chi direction.

What objects will make Chi slow down or be absorbed?

A heavy object, such as a sculpture or stones like those used in a Chinese garden, will absorb energy and/or force energy to move around it.

The various uses of color.

What else? Your intuition will give you other object and placement ideas that can modify Chi flow in logical and decorative ways.

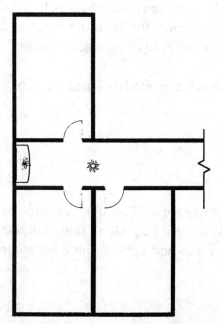

What if Chi is stagnating in an area like a dead end corridor? What if a hall is too dark or narrow? Chi will be squeezed so that it moves too slowly and doesn't reach other areas. This condition may create abdominal problems or cause pregnant women to have difficult deliveries. Get Chi moving.

Just don't put one of the above solutions in the corridor. Consider all traditional and Earth Design principles that are energetically beautifying.

What is the proper scale for a mirror on the back wall? Is there enough space to put a console underneath the mirror? Can you place a silk flower arrangement or sculpture of an animal on the console? Consider the elemental representations. What color should the flowers be? What material and shape should the vase be? Should the sculpture be made of bronze (*Metal)* or ceramic (*Earth)*?

Before hanging a crystal, consider whether or not the corridor is dark

A light would help to move Chi and make it easier to walk through.

Do you have the height to hang a lighting fixture that has crystal pendants? What is the height of the fixture? Will it hang too low? A good rule to remember is to never let a fixture that you walk under hang below standard door height, 6 feet 8 inches.

Does the fixture have beveled or refracted glass to also move Chi? What color is the glass? Does the fixture have exposed metal trim? Do you need special bulbs to avoid negative glare?

Earth Design decisions are multi-dimensional.

Doors

Using the body analogy again, doors are the line of demarcation between spaces, like the valves in our veins that help blood flow. Interior doors should swing inward into the room and open so they lay against the wall.[12]

---

[12] In an office, fire doors usually swing out, as required by local building codes. Architects design fire doors to allow proper pedestrian circulation by providing unobstructed passage in case of an emergency.

Contrary doors that swing into the center of a space against the natural flow restrict Chi from entering. Additionally, contrary doors do not allow you to comfortably enter the room, they limit furniture layout, and they are a safety hazard because you can't see who you are hitting with the door. Please try to change the door swing, or if this change is not possible, place a mirror on the wall in the location where the door should swing in order for energy to be reflected back into the room.

 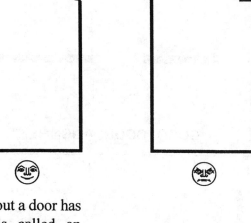

An opening without a door has no voice and is called an *empty door*. For Chi to flow properly, the opening must be defined. Recognize that the threshold is a transition into another area. Give the door a tongue by painting the jamb an accent color or by hanging a crystal, beads, lace, and/or ribbon. Use your creativity. This sketch has nine crystal balls hanging from nine centimeter red cords. The number nine[13] and the color red are auspicious.

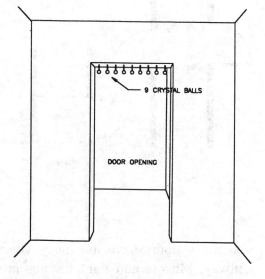

9 CRYSTAL BALLS

DOOR OPENING

---

[13]   Nine is the highest single numerical digit. Did you notice the price of the book? 2+4+2+1=9. Why is red the most sacred color?

Doors need to be aligned for Chi to have a direct channel to flow through. Improper flow is similar to a kink in a water hose. Since doors are symbolic of our mouths, when they are in alignment, they can speak when facing each other, allowing good communication.

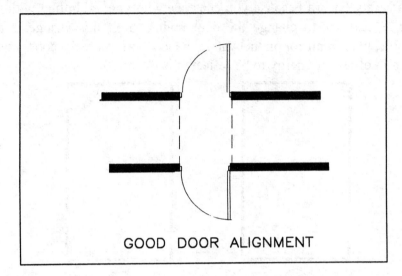

GOOD DOOR ALIGNMENT

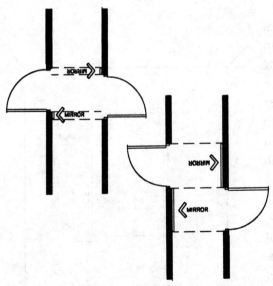

Biting doors cause conflict with their improper alignment. This situation is solved by adding reflective surfaces to either side of the doors to redirect Chi. In a business office, if mirrors are inappropriate, try using another feature, such as signage indicating the function or the name of the person that occupies the room, to catch the eye.

Too many doors have too many voices, as in the typical bedroom hallway. Mirrors and light fixtures provide excellent and functional solutions. It may be aesthetically appropriate to mirror the entire face of the door and wall, as in the following bathroom and bedroom example.

Mirrors will redirect Chi, open up a corridor that is too narrow, keep abundance from being washed away, and be used for getting dressed. A crystal chandelier will also be functional, as it illuminates space, directs Chi, and is a pleasing decorative element.

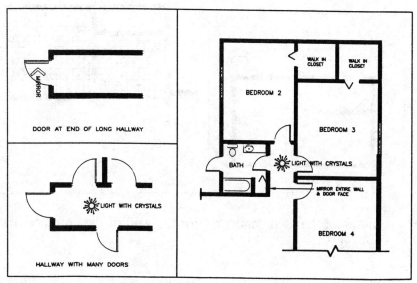

Arguing doors, or awkwardly placed doors, occur when doors open into each other. The typical application is a linen or air conditioner/water heater type closet. The easiest solution is to change the closet door to a bifold. To allow air and Chi to circulate so sheets stay fresh or allow heat to escape from equipment, consider using a louvered bifold. If the door is painted the same color as the wall, it will almost disappear, allowing important features greater prominence.

Interior Structural Conditions

Apartments sometimes have emotionally restrictive configurations. In this example, the entry is too narrow so that guests, and most importantly, the occupants feel squeezed when entering, which leaves no potential for expansion.

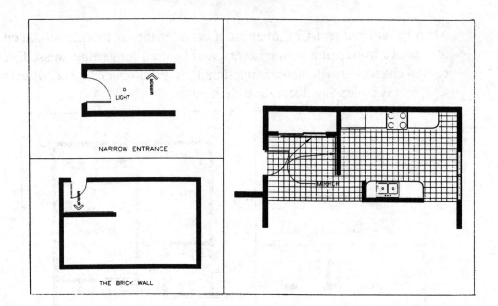

In the top left schematic, mirror the wall of the entrance that is too narrow.

In the other drawings, occupants subconsciously will feel they are always running into a *brick wall*. The solutions may be to:

> Knock down the brick wall, provided the rest of the layout will be functional.

> I do not suggest knocking down the wall for this sketch because it would be unattractive to walk right into the kitchen. Additionally, Chi would blow right out the breakfast room window or down the kitchen sink, not through to the rest of the apartment.

In the bottom left schematic, mirror the brick wall, or hang a mirror appropriate to the rest of the design.

> My Earth Design solution would be to mirror the left wall, including the face of the closet and the brick wall. That way, the closet disappears, and both elevations become a unified entry vestibule. It is clean design, looks good, and solves both the Chi and the frustration of being stuck.

A *split view* is a condition similar to a brick wall, except that only half of the vista is blocked. This situation may not affect Chi as badly, but it may cause physical or emotional problems. When it occurs, relationship problems or splitting headaches are the typical symptoms. To adjust the energetics of a split view, consider what you can you do to aesthetically focus both eyes on the same side.

Just like doors and windows, stairs are also Chi channels. A curved, graceful stairway is best because it follows the movement of Chi. The position of the stairs should be an asset that enables Chi access to the entire house. If the stair is right in front of the entry or directly at the mouth of another opening, Chi will flow into that space without having a chance to circulate throughout the other areas.

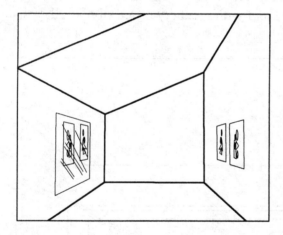

Beams, slanted walls or ceilings, and sharp angles may sometimes make a space feel oppressive. With all you have learned about energy, you will know if you have a space where Chi is squeezed.

Feel the energy in your body!

In a room with a slanted wall or ceiling that creates an irregular and unbalanced shape, it is best to hang a decorative mirror, or mirror the entire wall opposing the slant. The reflection will give the illusion that the space does not have such a constrictive angle. The area will appear more open and will reduce the oppressive feeling.

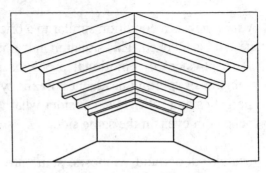

If you have enough height, repetitive beams that are not too large are favorable. They are reminiscent of the rhythms in nature, like the ripples on a lake or the veining in a leaf.

When the ceiling is too low or there are heavy structural beams, the occupants will not feel comfortable. The beam or low ceiling will feel as if it will crash down, and the heaviness in the air will be stifling.

The best solutions for oppressive beams are to either make them disappear by finishing them in the same material as the rest of the ceiling, to up-light them, or to accent them with greenery or red ribbons. Try to give them an uplifted feeling.

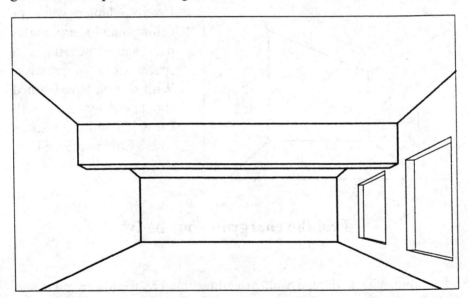

Do not put any furniture right underneath a beam. If possible, lay the room out as if it were two individual spaces separated by the beam. If this solution is not considered, the beam will separate the space physically and subconsciously regardless. In the above drawing, visualize the following conditions:

Clients will not feel comfortable in an executive's office that has a beam above the desk. The beam cuts the relationship and prohibits trust from developing.

A married couple that has a beam over the bed running length-wise, head to toe, will have marital problems because they will always be separated.

A beam running across the bed will cut the body in half, and may cause health problems.

What about secret arrows? In this example, look how the hard edge points directly at the door. What if there were a hard edge from a badly placed square column? You could soften the corner with a plant, a sculpture, or even a fish tank. Put a mirror up so the secret arrow is reflected back to itself, thereby causing its own demise. If it is a child's room, you can use an over-sized stuffed animal as a decoration.

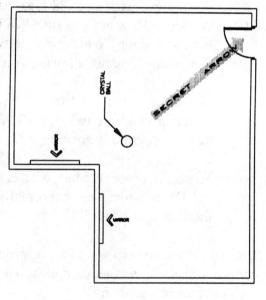

Be creative and remember to balance the missing hole on the other side.

What happens when Chi is not flowing as it should? What happens when the living room, where you lovingly and generously entertain your family and friends, does not breathe? What happens when the kitchen, the place for nourishment and nurturing, doesn't breathe? How do these conditions affect you? Which of your life situations: marriage, children, people who help you, self-cultivation, career, wealth, health, or position in society, is being choked?

Consider the effects of the following:

> Low ceilings may put pressure on your head, causing headaches . . . or worse. They may depress and oppress you, limiting your potential. A low ceiling in your office limits your ability to create.

> In a hall with many doors, there are too many views. When energy is equally distributed to each door in a hall, each personality occupying a room will not feel threatened. Personality conflicts will be minimized because each individual will be more understanding and respectful of the other's opinions.

> A dead end, stagnant Chi area, or brick wall represents blockage. How are you stuck? What barriers need to be broken through? What opportunities are you missing? Is there something not allowing you to see?

> Narrow corridors constrict and limit. How is the squeeze affecting your internal organs? What happens when the veins in your body are clogged?

> When Chi moves too fast, what is it that you can't hold on to? Do relationships, opportunity, or money just pass through your hands?

Did your intuition help you to recognize something that will affect you and your specific energetic applications? What is represented by the various areas in your home?

The Kitchen is the nourishing part of house that allows you access to money. Money is nurturing, and the water in the kitchen represents wealth. The kitchen is the place that can affect your digestion and your nervous system as well, due to all the electrical equipment.

If the kitchen were close to the entry, you may be food oriented and have a hard time eating properly or controlling your weight. Guests would often come over to eat. It is not good to have the kitchen located in the center of the house or in the primary path of Chi, where wealth could easily be washed down the sink.

The Bedroom requires soft Chi flow for the regeneration of your body and sacred relationships. It is the place where you regain your strength. Your health could suffer without proper Chi.

If the bedroom were close to the entry, you might feel tired much of the time and rarely feel completely rested. Even without others in the house, you might not be fully at ease because of the subconscious lack of privacy.

The Study/Office is the space that signifies stimulation, creativity, and innovation. If the study were close to the entry, you might be a work-a-holic or bookworm. You could have trouble honoring yourself with off time, even with the understanding of how important it is to your well-being.

The Living Room should be close to the entry because it is usually the most expansive space. Good feelings of family and friends should circulate in this area.

The Foyer is the transitional space that allows you to breathe in the sacred energy of your environment while shedding outside influences.

Even if you do not have a foyer, I recommend that you create a small space just inside the front door. In the previous sketch with the mirrored brick wall, there is just enough space to stand. I recommend that upon entering, take whatever time you need to make an energetic change in your being.

The Bathroom represents financial opportunity and *internal plumbing*. If a bathroom were proximate to the entry, Chi would not have a chance to circulate through the house because it would go right down the toilet. Financial opportunities, money, and whatever you do to enhance your health and harmony might also get flushed.

A bathroom should not be in the center of the house for the same reasons as the kitchen. If this undesirable location cannot be helped, keep the door closed and/or mirror the walls inside so Chi will bounce around and find its way back out.

What would happen if you put a door with a mirror on the rooms that were unfavorably positioned? Right, Chi would be reflected away from the unfavorably located room.

furniture Placement

Furnishings and equipment should *always* be positioned so that the person sitting in the chair, lying on the bed, or boiling rice on the stove has a clear view of the door. By being able to see someone walking into the space, you will not be startled, thus affording you greater comfort.

I call this the *Jesse James Syndrome.* Jesse would never sit with his back to the door! How do you feel when you are startled from behind? Jumpy? Your task or relaxation is interrupted, causing disharmony on all levels. By positioning furniture with this principle in mind, everyone will be less nervous, more relaxed, happier, and easier to live with. Your blood pressure won't go up and affect your health. You won't put unnecessary stress on yourself or on the people around you.

If for any reason this optimum positioning of furniture cannot be accomplished, hang a mirror so the entry may be appropriately seen. For example, position the mirror in the bedroom at the height suitable to view the door from either a sitting or lying down position in bed.

Your furniture layout should be done with consideration of how people and Chi move through the space. Furniture should not be positioned so that a door cannot open properly. Cramped furnishings look and feel restrictive, and Chi does not circulate properly. It is uncomfortable and potentially hazardous.

Furniture layout must be appropriate to the task.

**Furniture needs to be dimensioned in proportion
to each other and to the size of the room.**

The Kitchen layout includes the range, sink, and refrigerator. Notice the triangular relationship in the sketches. Keep in mind that the entry doors must be easily visible from all the work centers.

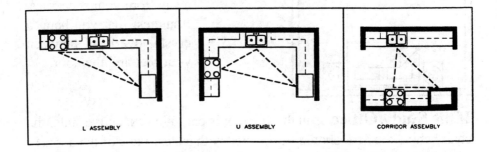

L ASSEMBLY   U ASSEMBLY   CORRIDOR ASSEMBLY

The stove is one of the most important pieces of equipment in the home. Like Laura Esquivel's heroine of the book, *Like Water for Chocolate*, who ceremoniously prepares food for the lover she will never have, love, sensitivity, and sensuousness are expressed through eating food that has been honored by the sacredness of the stove and the cook.

The burners are a symbol of financial prosperity. Use all of them so money comes from many different sources. If you want to increase your resources, put a mirror behind the stove and double the amount of burners.

Many combination stove units have a microwave on top. Your instincts should tell you that the microwave not only sends a beam of radiation into your head but has a heaviness on top that oppresses the beneficial influence. Traditionally it is said that this situation may cause bad luck. Hanging a crystal ball about head level should minimize the energetics. As it will not solve the radiation problem, if you must use a microwave, please stand back while it is in use.

In the Bedroom try to orient the bed in the middle of a room so that the energy flows around you. I could never understand the platform design trend. Toes always get stubbed and you may fall off. It is less hazardous to have your bed off the floor, allowing Chi to also circulate underneath. This is the same premise previously discussed: *wrap your body* in the nurturing effects of Chi.

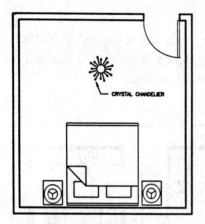

Chi may flow out of your body through your feet if they point toward the door. So as to not be pulled away from your successes, I suggest that you hang a crystal overhead between your feet and the door.

If the Study/Office is in the home or is part of an executive suite, the chair behind the desk should be oriented with a clear view of the door. In a residential office, perhaps there will be enough area for a sleeper sofa so that the room can double as a guest room.

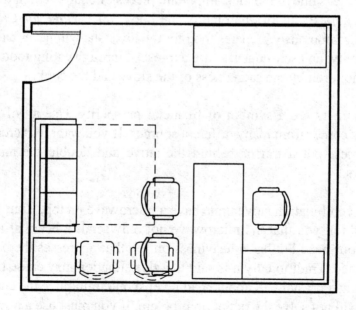

In the Living Room or waiting area in an office, the furniture should be oriented so that the majority of seats have a view of the entry. The aesthetic combination of such pieces as sofas, love seats, and individual club chairs should be arranged in comfortable conversation groups.

As a gracious host, expect your guest to choose the *seat of honor*, indicated by an asterisk (*). This seat is typically oriented with the best view of the door. It may be one of the positions on a sofa or a feature chair, depending on the particular furniture and layout. To assist in furnishing selection and layout, consider the following observation: unless there is not enough seating, it is highly unlikely that three people will ever sit abreast on a single sofa, or two people on a love seat.

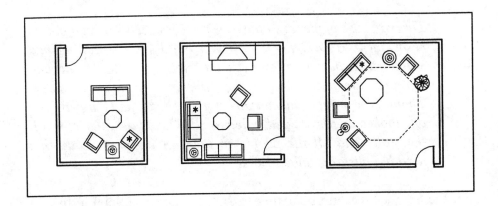

In the Dining Room the traditional formal layout is to have the host and hostess at opposite ends of a rectangular table. Rectangular tables work best because dining rooms are typically rectangular. Round, oval, square, and soft-cornered auspicious octagonal *Bagua* shaped tables are also nice if the space is appropriate to allow proper pedestrian and Chi circulation. If there is only one host, it would be gracious to ask the guest of honor to sit at the end of the table that faces the entry. For practical reasons, the host/cook usually sits at the end closest to the kitchen.

The Foyer/Entry should be well illuminated and inviting without obstruction of any kind. The furniture should be sparse but important, perhaps a bench or console with a mirror above to enhance Chi flow.

Bathrooms should look as expensive as possible because they represent wealth. Try to not use dark colors that will tend to enclose the space. The toilet should be positioned furthest from the door, not only for psychological privacy but as a deterrent to flushing Chi. Fortunately, most architects lay bathrooms out appropriately.

If there is a layout problem, a mirror can be placed behind the toilet to deflect Chi. Please be careful about positioning mirrors in the bathroom. Consider all the people that may be using it; male or female, tall or short. Make sure they do not have to look at their reflection when they are busy. Respect that some people need privacy from themselves.

> *The worst use of mirrors I have ever experienced was in a public restroom in a Designer Showroom building. The ceiling had standard acoustical tiles over the stalls, and as an accent, mirrored tiles were hung in the walkway in front of the stalls. Though the mirror was not directly overhead, as I sat privately and looked up, the angled reflection displayed the interior of all the stalls and all the people in them. A designer made that dreadful mistake; unbelievable!*

For the obvious reason of *cooking waste,* it is not beneficial to have a bathroom proximate to the kitchen. Use the tools discussed so far for your intuitive cure.

In the Corporate Layout the same principles of Earth Design apply. The Corporate Layout is extremely important because it determines whether the business will be successful in maintaining an abundance of clients and a positive cash flow.

A complete Corporate Design Package requires the skill and talent of an Interior Architectural and (Earth) Interior Designer who have the necessary education and experience. Since many of my readers are in the work place, I will briefly describe the corporate design process and apply Earth Design principles. This description will be beneficial when you are working with a professional designer or if you try to design the space yourself.

While your ideas are critical to the design, I highly recommend that you use a professional. A competitive design fee is minimal compared to the possible costly mistakes. By hiring a professional, the job should be done quickly and right the first time. If you choose to do it yourself, you might create additional direct or indirect costs such as:

Lost business, while on the *design learning curve*, prevents you from doing the job where you are most expert. Time or business may be lost because of improper design, layout, or furnishings not specific to the tasks.

Construction layout problems and reconstruction due to local building code requirements, ADA (American Disabilities Act), or public and fire safety requirements.

Lost income caused by delays in construction, relocation, and other down time because of inexperienced coordination.

Space planning is the process of ascertaining appropriate wall partitions and furnishings appropriate to the architecture and to the specific requirements of the particular business. A designer will interview the executives and department managers to develop a *design profile* that outlines all the specific business needs.

The following issues should be addressed:

How many executives and required support staff are there?

How many other departments, how do they operate, and how many people per department? What are the specific jobs, or what furnishings and layout position will help each individual be most productive?

What are the filing and storage, computer, telephone, and mail room requirements?

How many conference rooms are required, and how many people attend the meetings?

Is there a multi-purpose room, a kitchen, or a lounge?

How does the *paper flow* between departments?

What are the projected growth and future needs of the company?

What is the specialized equipment? And so on . . .

As you can see, for optimum function this process is quite an undertaking. A professional has learned to assess this information quickly and transfer it on paper in a two-dimensional corporate space plan.

We, as spinning wheels of transformation, need to share the same Earth Design principles used in our homes so that our selected professional may apply them to our office environment because:

We want our corporate space to be aligned with the natural laws and to generate optimum abundance for our business efforts. We want to work smarter not harder!

As more harmonious beings, while we share our positive energy with each other, we make the process easier, and *fun*.

It introduces an *Added Dimension* to design, which will then be incorporated as part of the selected professional's design practice. What a Gift!

The most critical considerations are: the locations of the entry, president, and senior executives. The principals of the firm are the main source of business creativity and motivation. These locations need to be in accordance with Earth Design principles. When personal energetics are aligned with the spatial energetics and the area is laid out properly, the entire organization will benefit.

The location of the president and directors' offices should also signify authority and power. The offices should be positioned in an area with abundant Chi flow. While these offices should be the most important and impressive, there is a fine line to be considered. The president and senior staff should not be set apart or positioned in an overly commanding way that may intimidate employees or clients. When they are not subliminally separated from the *whole*, employees will feel like an integral part of the organization. Clients, the essence of business, will see the entire organization working in unity toward the common goals and objectives of the firm.

The following is an example of a good corporate layout.

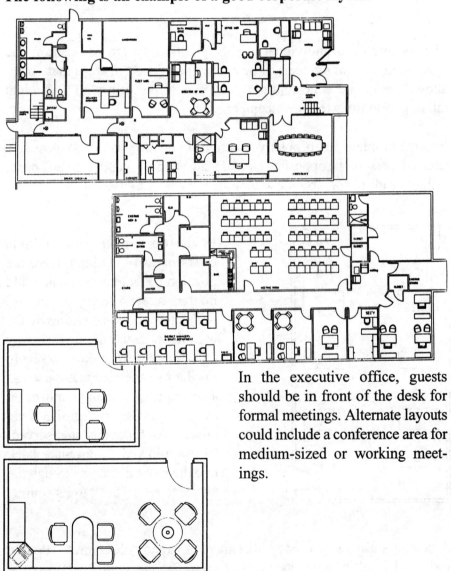

In the executive office, guests should be in front of the desk for formal meetings. Alternate layouts could include a conference area for medium-sized or working meetings.

The conference table desk, with a corner computer credenza, offers the executive the best of both arrangements. If the room is large enough, an area with lounge seating may be incorporated for less formal meetings.

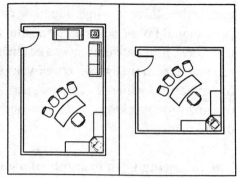

The success of an individual is also qualified by spatial position and location to other individuals. If people are positioned in areas that do not allow appropriate concentration, they cannot perform well and might miss opportunities for advancement.

Positive people give off positive energy. If you are positioned close to a negative person, the opposite is true. I suggest that you put a crystal paper weight or mirror on your desk to deflect the negativity.

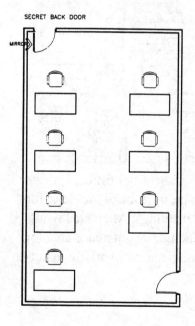

In the open plan with multiple desks or work stations, there are position considerations that could hinder careers from advancing. For example, people sitting by the back door are usually on their way out. The best solution is to secure the door so the area is not used as a corridor. By placing a mirror on the silenced voice of the *dead door,* two functions are served; Chi is allowed to circulate back into the room and pass through the mirror to return back to its source.

A person sitting in the entry or exit path cannot concentrate. People walking by will be a constant disturbance. The individual is also in the direct line of Chi. It blows right though without nurturing the space. The solution is to put a mirror that faces away from the person on both the credenza and the desk.

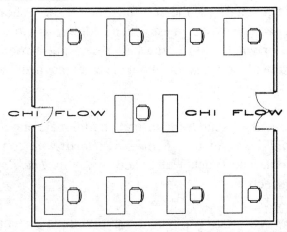

In the examples, if the desks are work stations surrounded by panels that are at least forty-two inches high, the head of the person is somewhat protected, and this situation does not present such a serious problem. I still suggest the use of mirrors. If you cannot use a mirror because of office politics, place the mirror in your drawer facing the problem area to symbolically deflect Chi.

Energetic Overlays

An overlay is a design term that is just as the name suggests. It is a sheet of tracing paper with Earth Design information (Feng Shui Horoscope, Western Astrology, Bagua, Chi Flow, and so on) overlaid on top of your floor plan. By looking at the overlays on top of each other, you will have all the information you need to make energetic Earth Design decisions.

Overlays are designer tools that help with various applications. Architects use them to plan mechanical, electrical, and structural systems, while interior designers use them to determine the layout and scale of furnishings.

Since most of my readers do not architecturally design their home or office, more than likely, the room configuration is already determined.

You are restricted to the existing room locations and the directions they face.[14] Without major reconstruction, the kitchen, bathrooms, master bedroom, living and dining rooms are already defined.

The overlays help you decide the best function for the rest of the spaces. In these cases, overlays will suggest which bedroom is more appropriate for each child or what room is the better den, guest room, or office. Overlays will provide information about the earth magnetics and personal energetics for all the rooms.

The energetic overlays come from different traditional Feng Shui schools. The *Directional Energies* and *Feng Shui Horoscope* come from the Compass School. The Black Hat School gives us *The Bagua* from a geomantic perspective.

As you review the overlays, you may find inconsistencies due to different interpretations. Earth Design borrows from them all, and I recommend that you consider all the options. Play with the overlays, and process them through your intuitive interpretation. As you remember, this process is no different from how geomancy was applied throughout history. After making your decisions, apply the cures, and set the intent with purposeful determination. Then let it go.

I have seen people go to extremes in this part of the evaluation. I have known people to put their beds in the living room---making entertaining interesting---or their dining table in the bedroom---nowhere near the kitchen---because of the overlay information. Can you begin to imagine the disharmony created?

Be realistic! Use the overlays to logically change the function by using traditional design principles according to the existing architecture. Use appropriate Earth Design to change the energetics where it is not logical to change the function.

---

[14] In the future, consider spatial energetics and good Chi flow, which are as important as the other determining factors, before moving.

Directional Energetics

The inherent energetics of a space are based upon the earth's magnetic fields. You learned in Chapter 3 what the Chinese have known from thousands of years of intuitive observation. They understood that long-term exposure to electromagnetic energy often caused disease and misfortune.

Similar to the western ancients who dispersed magnetic energy by locating their sacred structures on the crossing of ley lines, for the same reasons, the Chinese never positioned buildings directly on the dragon lines.

The basis of Compass School Feng Shui is to be in alignment with the natural earth magnetics. This alignment is determined by the direction your home or office faces.

With this information you can discover:

> The areas of best inherent energy.
>
> How to align with the directional energy to combine with your personal energetics as determined by your Feng Shui Horoscope.
>
> How to make appropriate modifications through the representations of the elemental cycles and conventional design ideas.

Through energetic modifications, personal alignment will be according to the natural magnetic forces to improve the quality of your life:

> **Mind:**   By promoting a greater sense of comfort, harmonized relationships, and the potential for greater wealth.
>
> **Body:**   By improving physical health.
>
> **Spirit:**   By improving the internal harmony affecting everything else.

The Compass School divides the magnetic energetics of a space into eight sections, represented by the cardinal and non-cardinal directions[15] determined by magnetic north. Chinese geomancers use a specialized compass called the *Lo Pan*. For our purposes, the better the compass, the more accurate the reading.

Directional energy is based upon the direction the house faces relative to the front door.

The front door, as you remember, is the mouth of the home, and the main source of Chi. Therefore, the front door location is the primary factor in determining the directional energies. To find the direction your house faces, go outside and stand with your back against the front door. The direction your eyes are looking is the direction your house is facing. With your back still against the door, what is the compass reading? If it reads southeast, your house faces southeast.

Suggestions:

Remove your watch or metal/magnetic jewelry. Make sure there is nothing such as a car or metal door in the immediate area to alter the compass reading.

Do several checks for accuracy because an improper reading will translate into improper information. Do a reading on the same line ten feet in front of the door and in several different areas of your house.

---

[15] Do you remember the geomantic representations of such directions as the sacred shape of a cross or the Native American's *power of the eight directions?*

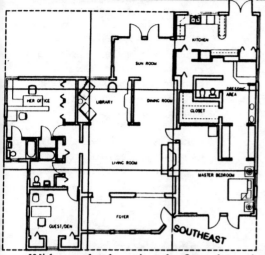

When you are comfortable with the compass reading, segment you space into eight[16] sections and label them with the appropriate directions. This process will help you to determine the inherent favorable or unfavorable qualities of each section or direction.

With your back against the front door, the house faces the direction your eyes are looking. When your front door is on an angle, as in this case, determine what direction the front of the house faces. This house faces South.

**Any area that occupies more than two/thirds of the
dimension of the room should be included in the grid.**

It may be a benefit that some areas, such as the northwest area in the above graphic, are not contained in the living part of the house. Do not worry if the sections of the grid divide the rooms.

As in nature's balance and the positive and negative earth's magnetic energies, every space will have either beneficial, *perceived* detrimental, or neutral energies. When you recognize the differences, perceived detrimental energies can be remedied, and neutral energies may be enhanced.

**Unfavorable areas are not bad areas.
They are opportunities to enhance your life!**

From the following graphic, select the appropriate grid represented by the direction your home faces.

---

16   Traditionally, the center is neither favorable nor unfavorable. Because the center is the sacred ninth section and the hub of the household, my intuition and observation suggest that this area is favorable.

Earth Design
The Added Dimension

For everyone, who wants Greater Health, Wealth & Happiness along with a more beautiful and functional environment!

Written by Jami Lin, a licensed professional interior designer, *Earth Design: The Added Dimension* (ISBN: 0-9643060-9-30) is simply outlined with practical, creative, and inexpensive ideas for decorating your home and office according to nature's perfection, proven to enhance abundance and well-being.

Earth Design is changing people's lives. Joseph Campbell would suggest that it is a tool for planning our environments so they support our personal mythology.

Similar to *The Celestine Prophesy*, the explanations of how and why the ancients incorporated Earth Design in their buildings are REAL. The popular best seller is an insightful story of its characters' awakening to their inner spirit, while Earth Design provides tangible tools that connect personal mythology or spirit to the substance and form of our physical space.

Called **Feng Shui** (fung sway) by the Chinese, Earth Design was used by the Greeks, Egyptians, Mayans, and throughout Europe to align their environments to the perfection of nature.

Through a cross-cultural and scientific foundation, Earth Design becomes a personal journey, from Stone Age to New Age, describing how the natural cycles were applied to ancient as well as current buildings.

Readers discover how to recognize and add the historically tested secrets of the earth to their environment. Brief references to Plato, Pythagoras, and such contemporary architects as Frank Lloyd Wright and Buckminster Fuller explain how the mythology of the earth can transform our space to support universal humanitarian needs.

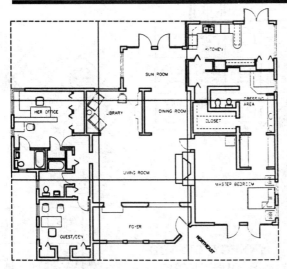

When you are comfortable with the compass reading, segment your space into eight[16] sections and label them with the appropriate directions. This process will help you to determine the inherent favorable or unfavorable qualities of each section or direction.

With your back against the front door, this house faces northeast. It is important to segment the entire structure according to this rule:

Any area that occupies more than two/thirds of the dimension of the room should be included in the grid.

It may be a benefit that some areas, such as the southeast area in the above graphic, are not contained in the living part of the house. Do not worry if the sections of the grid divide the rooms.

As in nature's balance and the positive and negative earth's magnetic energies, every space will have either beneficial, *perceived* detrimental, or neutral energies. When you recognize the differences, perceived detrimental energies can be remedied, and neutral energies may be enhanced.

Unfavorable areas are <u>not</u> bad areas.
They are opportunities to enhance your life!

From the following graphic, select the appropriate grid represented by the direction your home faces.

---

[16]   Traditionally, the center section is neither favorable nor unfavorable. Because the center is the sacred ninth section and the hub of the household, my intuition and observation suggest that this area is favorable.

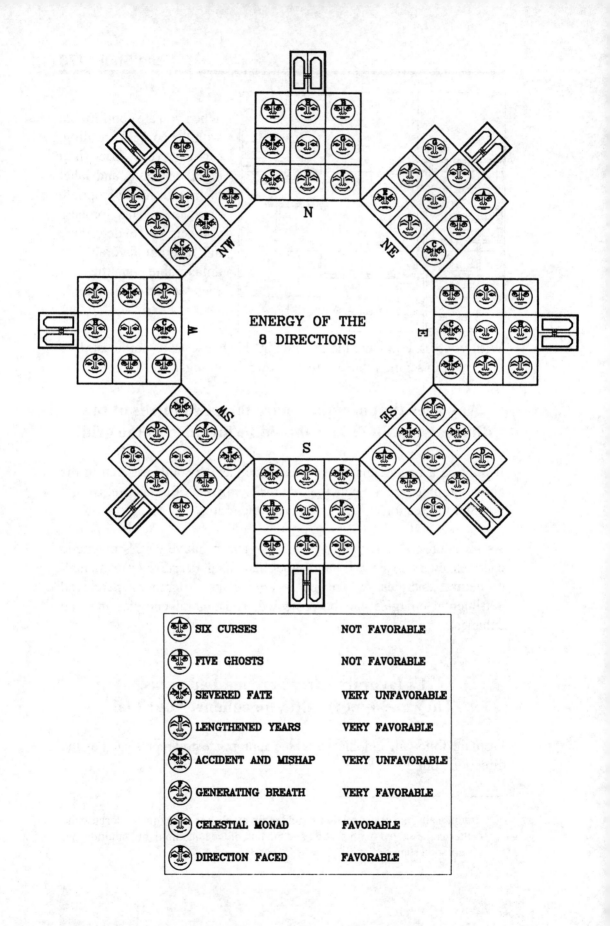

ENERGY OF THE
8 DIRECTIONS

SIX CURSES	NOT FAVORABLE
FIVE GHOSTS	NOT FAVORABLE
SEVERED FATE	VERY UNFAVORABLE
LENGTHENED YEARS	VERY FAVORABLE
ACCIDENT AND MISHAP	VERY UNFAVORABLE
GENERATING BREATH	VERY FAVORABLE
CELESTIAL MONAD	FAVORABLE
DIRECTION FACED	FAVORABLE

Energy of the Eight Directions

In *The Feng Shui Handbook*,[a] Derek Waters describes the traditional compass representations of the energetics. I have further interpreted these definitions based on my own Earth Design experience and added the comments in parentheses for further clarification.

A. Six Curses or the Seventh Curse:

This area foreshadows an unfavorable event. While it probably will be minor, it may be repeated seven times.

(Always respect this space for its possible potential. Either use it for storage, a guest room, or for a person having favorable attributes[17] in this area.)

B. Five Ghosts:

This is the area where embodied spirits may be present. The area may have a haunted feeling about it. Traditionally, this area may be reserved for family photographs or a shrine for protection. A room with the ancestors would be perfect to connect with their departed spirits.

(Through your power of Spirit, fill this space with love and light entities that support you. This is the area where you most easily may receive guidance from your *angels*. The space doesn't need to have any negative vibrations; it is up to you.)

---

[17]   Please see *Feng Shui Horoscope* section in this Chapter and *Astrology*, Chapter 6.

Try to determine the emotional or spiritual reason that caused the unfavorable situation in the first place. When you get to the root of the problem, the repetition of the curse will be avoided or the conditions will lessen. Aren't we here to do it until we get it right?

C. Severed Fate:

This area may signify the end of life. It is not appropriate to spend a lot of time in this area, especially if you are recovering from an illness. Use this area for storage. Often, buildings designed according to The Compass School are deliberately designed without this section.

(This concept is in direct opposition to filling the missing whole. As the Gemini messenger, I share this information. My personal experience has the holistic conviction that the whole will always have greater value. However, should this information resonate as truth, and the space must be occupied, I suggest decorating it with objects that remind you of the beauty and grace of life. Use talismans and accessories that make you feel good. Through your personal power, you have the capacity to protect yourself.)

D. Lengthened Years:

This area is perfect for living, working, or sleeping.

(Can this be your master bedroom?)

E. Accident and Mishap:

This area is susceptible to accidents and injury. Take all safety precautions and always be aware in this space. It is not recommended for such areas as the kitchen or bathroom, which are prone to mishaps. It is also not the ideal bedroom for a child.

(Be careful and respectful. Use this space for storage, a guest room, or for a person that has favorable Feng Shui Horoscope or Western Astrological attributes.)

F. Generating Breath:

This area is the breath of the house, full of vitality and creativity.

G. Celestial Monad:

This area traditionally neutralizes unfavorable energies. It is a good location for people who have been ill or have experienced misfortune, a perfect area to be rejuvenated on all levels.

(This is ideal for the bedroom, to make love, to dream, and to regenerate. It's a great place for meditation and affirmation.)

H. The Direction faced by the front door.

Welcome. This is a favorable area.

(Breathe the Chi force when you walk into your sacred space; this is your sanctuary!)

Exercise: *Divide your home or office into nine sections. Determine the favorable or perceived unfavorable areas by the direction your front door is facing. Overlay the faces onto your floor plan. While it is important to wait until you overlay your personal horoscope, begin to think about how to change the energetics by using Earth Design intuition and intention. Use the plan that follows to help you.*

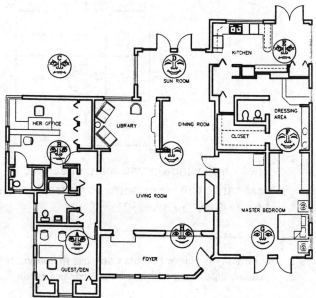

If a room appears to have two different energies, the area will take on the characteristics of both. It will be easy to recognize the dominating energy. As in the example, the tub and toilet area share both Generating Breath and Accident/Mishap energy. While she needs to be careful, the lady of the house reads and regenerates in the bath tub. Watch what happens when you look at her personal horoscope.

feng Shui Horoscope

It is my understanding that Chinese Astrology has been coveted throughout the ages and that much of it has been lost over the centuries. I speculate it is as complex as Western Astrology, but it is hard to verify because there are so few experts, especially ones that speak English.

For Earth Design, you need to know your natal element to determine the areas that are best suited to you. With this information, you can combine your personal energetics with the inherent directional energetics of your home.

There are three steps:

1.   The directions represent one of the five elements. Label an overlay with the elements as indicated in the chart below.

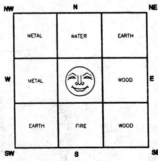

2.   Look in the appropriate male or female column, and locate the year[18] that you were born. Is your Natal Element: *Wood, Fire, Metal, Earth*, or *Water*?

---

[18]   If your birthday is before February 5th, use the previous year. February 5th is the approximate date of the Chinese New Year or first day of spring.

Personal Natal Element

1925-1975

YEAR	MALE	FEMALE
1925	Wood	Wood
1926	Earth	Wood
1927	Water	Earth
1928	Fire	Metal
1929	Earth	Metal
1930	Metal	Earth
1931	Metal	Fire
1932	Earth	Water
1933	Wood	Earth
1934	Wood	Wood
1935	Earth	Wood
1936	Water	Earth
1937	Fire	Metal
1938	Earth	Metal
1939	Metal	Earth
1940	Metal	Fire
1941	Earth	Water
1941	Wood	Earth
1943	Wood	Wood
1944	Earth	Wood
1945	Water	Earth
1946	Fire	Metal
1947	Earth	Metal
1948	Metal	Earth
1949	Metal	Fire
1950	Earth	Water
1951	Wood	Earth
1952	Wood	Wood
1953	Earth	Wood
1954	Water	Earth
1955	Fire	Metal
1956	Earth	Metal
1957	Metal	Earth
1958	Metal	Fire
1959	Earth	Water
1960	Wood	Earth
1961	Wood	Wood
1962	Earth	Wood
1963	Water	Earth
1964	Fire	Metal
1965	Earth	Metal
1966	Metal	Earth
1967	Metal	Fire
1968	Earth	Water
1969	Wood	Earth
1970	Wood	Wood
1971	Earth	Wood
1972	Water	Earth
1973	Fire	Metal
1974	Earth	Metal
1975	Metal	Earth

1976-2026

YEAR	MALE	FEMALE
1976	Metal	Fire
1977	Earth	Water
1978	Wood	Earth
1979	Wood	Wood
1980	Earth	Wood
1981	Water	Earth
1982	Fire	Metal
1983	Earth	Metal
1984	Metal	Earth
1985	Metal	Fire
1986	Earth	Water
1987	Wood	Earth
1988	Wood	Wood
1989	Earth	Wood
1990	Water	Earth
1991	Fire	Metal
1992	Earth	Metal
1993	Metal	Earth
1994	Metal	Fire
1995	Earth	Water
1996	Wood	Earth
1997	Wood	Wood
1998	Earth	Wood
1999	Water	Earth
2000	Fire	Metal
2001	Earth	Metal
2002	Metal	Earth
2003	Metal	Fire
2004	Earth	Water
2005	Wood	Earth
2006	Wood	Wood
2007	Earth	Wood
2008	Water	Earth
2009	Fire	Metal
2010	Earth	Metal
2011	Metal	Earth
2012	Metal	Fire
2013	Earth	Water
2014	Wood	Earth
2015	Wood	Wood
2016	Earth	Wood
2017	Water	Earth
2018	Fire	Metal
2019	Earth	Metal
2020	Metal	Earth
2021	Metal	Metal
2022	Earth	Metal
2023	Metal	Earth
2024	Metal	Fire
2025	Earth	Water
2026	Wood	Earth

3. Use your Natal Element to determine if the eight areas are personally favorable or unfavorable though the generative and destructive cycles.

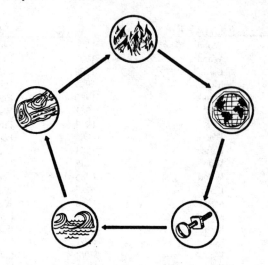

The generative order of the elements.

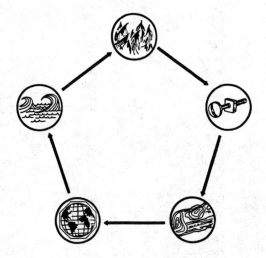

The destructive order of the elements

By using the chart below and symbols (++, +, --, or -) in each section, you can easily recognize the degree of favorability or unfavorability in the areas of your house.

<u>SYMBOL KEY</u>

1.   Location Element generates Natal Element
very favorable   ++

2.   Location Element destroys Natal Element
very unfavorable   --

3.   Location Element matches Natal Element
favorable   +

4.   Natal Element generates Location Element
unfavorable   -

5.   Natal Element destroys Location Element
favorable   +

Let's do two samples, using the owners of the home we have been evaluating. (Take a deep breath; it is not as complicated as it appears.) Just ask yourself these questions as you move around the sections:

Is the direct relationship between your *natal* and *location* in the destructive or generative cycle?

What is location *doing* to natal or what is natal *doing* to location?

Is it favorable or unfavorable?

Husband (Y):   Birth Year '55   Fire Element
Working clockwise (starting in the North)

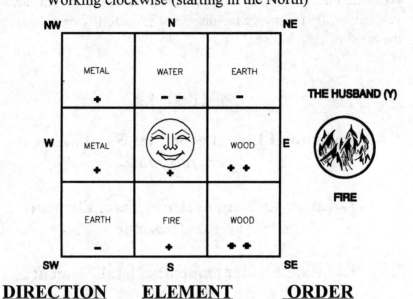

#	DIRECTION	ELEMENT	ORDER
2	North	Water	--
	Water Destroys Fire/Location Destroys Natal		
4	North-East	Earth	-
	Fire Generates Earth/Natal Generates Location		
1	East	Wood	++
	Wood Generates Fire/Location Generates Natal		
1	South-East	Wood	++
	Wood Generates Fire /Location Generates Natal		
3	South	Fire	+
	Fire Matches Fire/Natal Matches Location		
4	South-West	Earth	-
	Fire Generates Earth/Natal Generates Location		
5	West	Metal	+
	Fire Destroys Metal/Natal Destroys Location		
5	North-West	Metal	+
	Fire Destroys Metal/Natal Destroys Location		

Wife (X): **Birth Year '59** **Water Element**

Working clockwise (starting in the North)

NW	N	NE
METAL ✦ ✦	WATER ✦	EARTH -- --
W METAL ✦ ✦	(face) ✦	WOOD - E
EARTH -- --	FIRE ✦	WOOD -
SW	S	SE

THE WIFE (X)

WATER

#	DIRECTION	ELEMENT	ORDER
3	North	Water	+
	Water Matches Water/Natal Matches Location		
2	North-East	Earth	--
	Earth Destroys Water/Location Destroys Natal		
4	East	Wood	-
	Water Generates Wood /Natal Generates Location		
4	South-East	Wood	-
	Water Generates Wood/Natal Generates Location		
5	South	Fire	+
	Water Destroys Fire/Natal Destroys Location		
2	South-West	Earth	--
	Earth Destroys Water/Location Destroys Metal		
1	West	Metal	++
	Metal generates Water /Location Generates Natal		
1	North-West	Metal	++
	Metal Generates Water/Location Generates Metal		

Now overlay Your **Natal Energetics** and the **Directional Energetics** (front door location) on your floor plan to have a completely personalized energetic evaluation of your home.

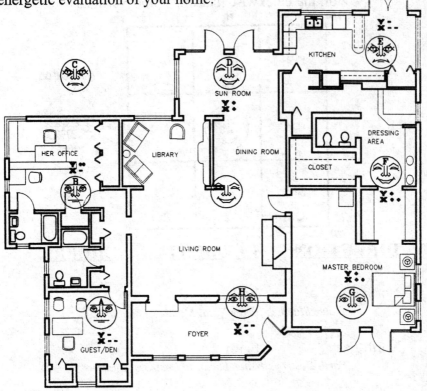

Y represents the Husband's personal Natal Energies

X represents the Wife's personal Natal Energies

After you do this analysis, it will be easier for you to decide the best function for the individual people in each room. For example:

A. Six Curses:

> This area is not very beneficial for either the husband or wife, so it is perfect for a guest room. Not a lot of time is spent here, which reduces the potential for setbacks. There is a mirror on the wall facing the front window to allow the beneficial energy of the canal across the street to fill the room. With the mirror, the balance of generative furnishings and finishes, and the protecting influence of the accessories, the space is suitable for someone, such as a child, with complimentary energies.

B. Five Ghosts:

Architecturally, this is the logical place for the wife's office, where she runs a small business. Remember, just because this is the area of potential spirits, it doesn't mean they are harmful influences. However, this is not the best area for her energetically, further solutions and analysis will follow.

C. Severed Fate:

This exterior space contains the pool pump. It is heavily landscaped to conceal and absorb the noise from the pump. The plants also provide protection from the Severed Fate and keep it from entering the office through the window. The missing whole is filled with the heavy equipment.

D. Lengthened Years:

Perfect! The sun fills this room with light and delight. The western sunlight and heat are controlled by solar window treatments. The room is used for relaxing, meditation, and Tai Chi.

E. Accident and Mishap:

Though there is a mirror doubling the burners and enabling a view of the rear, this kitchen provides its owners with a great excuse to go out to eat!

F. Generating Breath:

Now you see why she really loves the tub!! Although this section crosses into the *Accident and Mishap* area, her personal Chi adds power to the energy of the space.

G. Celestial Monad:

Ah, Perfect!

H. The Direction facing the front door.

Again, the mouth directs Chi from the canal across the street to fill the house with energizing, nurturing, and opportunities for abundance.

Regarding problem spots, such as the energies in the west office, further evaluation will determine what can be done to remedy the situation. Do a micro-study by dividing the usable area of the office into the nine sections, the same way you did for the entire house. This study will determine the best location for the furnishings, proportionate to how much time is spent in each of the sections. With proper functional and elementally appropriate furnishings, finishes, and accessories, the unfavorable energetics will be minimized, if not completely modified, to have neutral or even positive effects.

First, decide the direction the room faces (west) and do an overlay with the inherent earth energies. As this space is the wife's office, use her Feng Shui Horoscope to determine the best layout specific to her needs.

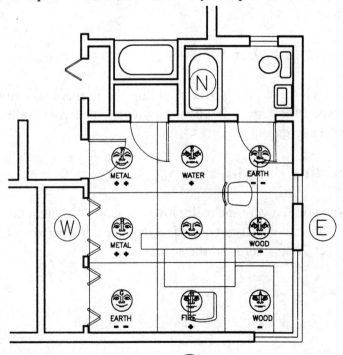

Although there is a great deal of furniture in this space, the layout provides a fully functional working environment. The bookcases are four feet high to give her privacy while she is seated and to allow Chi flow.

Remember, Earth Design is three-dimensional.

A. Six Curses:

The two-drawer lateral file cabinet is located in this area (storage). It is low enough to sit underneath the window sill, so as not to hinder Chi or natural light. The tops can be used as a surface for reference books or a fax machine.

B. Five Ghosts:

Her angels and guides are right overhead, just as they should be. Her **Natal Element** (Water) *Destroys* the **Location Element** (Fire), so this is a positive area in which she can be productive.

C. Severed Fate:

The bookcases and lateral files are positioned[19] in this location. No one occupies the space to pick up that energy.

D. Lengthened Years:

The part-time assistant sits at the secondary work area. The assistant is not affected by the wife's personal energy. In order for her not to be *on the lookout for Jesse James*, a decorative mirror (in the auspicious Bagua shape) is placed just above eye level so that in the reflection, she can detect movement from someone walking through the door. The mirror also serves to bring Chi from the rest of the house. The door to the bathroom is kept closed so creative wealth will not be flushed.

---

[19] These files are used to divide the space in a functional way. The fronts of the bookcases and lateral files are accessible from the appropriate sides, providing both privacy and storage at the same time.

If this layout were in a public office building, the location of this desk would not be acceptable. The assistant would not feel secure (even with the mirror) with her back exposed. Given that this is a private home, and she knows who is in the house at all times, the mirror and layout provide her with a comfortable work station.

E. Accident and Mishap:

Nothing is located there.

F. Generating Breath and H. The Entry:

The space is full of possibility. What wonderful potential can come out of this space!

G. Celestial Monad:

There is nothing in this area.

**Notice how logical design layout and energetics of
Earth Design are combined.**

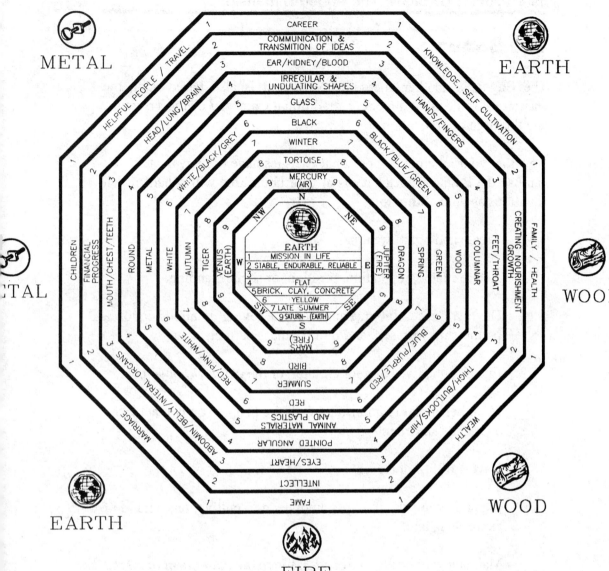

WATER

METAL

EARTH

METAL

WOOD

EARTH

WOOD

FIRE

1. LIFE SITUATION

2. SYMBOLISM

3. BODY PARTS

4. SHAPE

5. MATERIAL

6. COLOR

7. SEASON

8. ANIMAL

9. CHINESE PLANET (ASTROLOGICAL)

The Bagua

The Bagua

The Bagua is another energetic overlay. It is also based upon the energetics of the eight directions, traditional Chinese *I Ching* Trigrams, and the front door location.

Now that your inherent and personal energies have been evaluated, you can use the Bagua to locate areas in your house that will enhance such situations as your ability to:

Create and retain wealth,

Acquire fame, reputation, position, or social standing,

Have a successful marriage and a loving relationship or a partnership with self, and/or a business partner,

Enhance the lives of your children or the *child within you,*

Have beneficial relationships with the people you contact, such as friends and clients,

Have a fulfilling career,

Expand yourself through knowledge, cultivation, and self expression, and

Maintain your health to live a full life *to the attainment of all the other gifts of living.*

When all these situations are fulfilling the various aspects of your life, you are in balance with the *whole.* **You have the potential of being all that you can be.** When you feel lacking, or if you have the desire to encourage greater abundance in any area, use the Bagua to decide which location(s) to modify the energies.

After determining the life situations you wish to alter, overlay the Bagua on top of your floor plan. You can find the areas of your home that represent the various life situations.

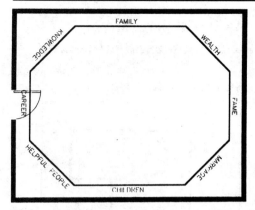

The *Career* face of the octagon is always parallel to and inside the front wall.

If the plan is not a regular rectangle, stretch the octagon proportionate to the layout. These rectangular-shaped homes have a *missing hole* or *Gua.* Each Gua is one of the eight triangles that make up the sacred geometry of the octagon.[20]

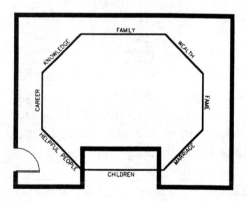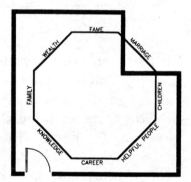

As shown, part of the Bagua is outside the structure, meaning that it is possible that the missing Gua will affect the represented life situation. (For example, if a couple chooses not to have children, the left example may be fine. If the individual has strong Chi, his/her inner child may not be an issue). The other consideration of adding the missing dimension will still need to be satisfied. In the example on the right, it may be difficult to find or keep a mate unless remedies are taken.

---

[20] Remember, the Bagua is a sacred life circle. It is the spinning wheel that stabilizes the balance and harmonics of our lives with the universal powers.

Personal Chi strength will determine
the proportional effect of environmental influences.

Positive influences will always be effective.

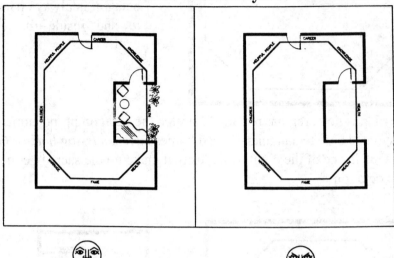

The above example shows the possibility that the occupants may be unhealthy. **This is priority one!** If you are not healthy, or if you are *dead* (either physically, emotionally, or spiritually), the other life situations are irrelevant. Cures for the missing life situation are the same as for filling the missing dimension. What solutions do you already know?

If there is not a door to the outside in this area, remember to leave an opening from the exterior as a walkway. Either the walkway or door into the house will provide healthy Chi flow. Plants must be healthy and without disease or pests. Healthy plants equal healthy energy.

Install a courtyard fountain or pond with lily pads and fish.

Install a big picture window in the room.

Let as much natural light and air from your new courtyard into your house for healing energy.

Install a ceiling fan. When it is on a moderate speed, healing Chi will flow thorough the rest of the house.

Put a fish tank or plants (or such representations of living things as a painting or sculpture) in the health area of the bedroom.

Put a mirror opposite the door in the rooms where you spend a lot of time to encourage healing Chi to enter.

Go into your courtyard and get a healing sun tan, but don't forget to use sunscreen.

What else? For those of you presented with this challenge, you know what to do.

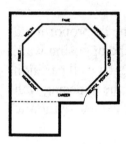 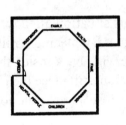 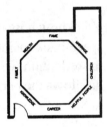

In the above examples, if a wing of the house is **less than half the width or length of the entire structure, it is considered a positive addition.**

Moving from left to right, starting with the left sketch, this house will increase study ability and the opportunities for scholarship. In the center sketch, an increase of wealth and financial opportunity may be expected. And in the one on the right, there will be a long and stable marriage.

A house with a boot or a *cleaver-shaped* plan and a disproportional wing has unbalanced energetics. The area outside the Bagua is energetically separated from the rest of the structure. If the space is used as an office, there is a beneficial separation between work and family.

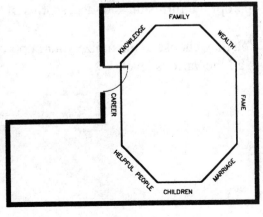

However, for the most part, there may be problems if remedies are not taken for the following areas:

> If the kitchen is outside the Bagua, the nourishing part of the house is separated, and the family will tend not to eat together, possibly growing apart.

> If the master bedroom is outside, one member may find that he/she prefers to sleep elsewhere.

> If the teenager's room is outside, he/she may tend to hang with the wrong crowd or be a discipline problem.

You know how to solve this situation already. Bring the disproportional space back inside the Bagua. By placing a mirror on the opposing wall, the reflection will bring the wing back inside the house. If a wall partition disallows the perfect reflection, still place the mirror on the opposing wall to bring the space back as close as possible for a physical and symbolic solution.

Notice the parts of the body shown on The Bagua at the beginning of this section. When a Gua is missing on your floor plan, there may be health problems in that part of an occupant's body. Use the same remedies as you would for any missing Gua.

It is possible to determine how and where to increase the potential of your selected *life situations* by using the Bagua to its full potential. This is done by choosing the life situations you want to enhance and adding appropriate furnishings or accessories in the represented areas.

You may choose to maximize your opportunities by making adjustments to all the various levels.

You can adjust:

The entire site for the macro/macro level,

The entire home for the macro level,

Each specific room for the micro level, and

Pieces of furniture that you spend a lot of time using for the micro/micro level.

Take full advantage of the Bagua overlay. Make adjustments on the lot, the whole house, the room, and/or your bed or desk.

For the couple who wants to strengthen their marriage:

On the Site:

They can install a light in the *marriage area* of the yard and surround it with plants having red, white, or pink flowers to illuminate the potential for deepening their relationship .

In the House:

If it is architecturally feasible, locate the master bedroom in the *marriage Gua (room)*. If this is not possible, symbolically put yourselves in the *marriage room* of the house and the *marriage area* of the master bedroom by hanging a loving photo of you both together. Consider a white or metal frame. Put a special love token on a red table cloth in the area or red silk roses in a white vase. Got it? Be careful not to over accessorize. One special piece in each place should be enough, especially when you set the intent as you place it.

In the Primary Room:

Select the room most appropriate to the life situation. The master bedroom is obviously the most appropriate room for marriage enhancement.

Your bed is the most important piece of furniture for this location and life situation. It is the place where your subconscious regenerates. Dream time allows the collective universe to help manifest your desires.

Is it possible to place the bed in the marriage position of the room? Make sure it is logically positioned not to block the closet entry or reduce necessary walking space. Be practical; otherwise it may become physically, emotionally, or subconsciously restrictive because of the other possible imbalances.

When it is not appropriate to move furnishings, the most useful way to modify the life situation energetics is to add appropriate accessories. This is the fun part. In this example, what can you add to the marriage area of the master bedroom that will represent your wonderful marriage? If you are not married and would like to be, what can you add to the marriage Gua to generate romance and partnership?

In a Secondary Room:

Select the next room where you spend the most time appropriate to the life situation. For me, this area would be my office; I would try to locate my desk there if architecturally feasible. Can you practically design the space so you spend most of your time in the marriage area? If not, hang a piece of art or place an accessory representative of your loving relationship.

On the Furniture:

Lay the Bagua on top of your furniture. Lay the *fame area* of the Bagua, on the *top* part of the piece of furniture.

In the primary room example, how about putting some rice thrown at your wedding under the mattress in the *marriage Gua* (upper right hand corner) of your bed?

In the secondary room example, can you put a picture of the two of you on the upper right-hand corner of your desk?

Notice how the Bagua is overlaid on the sample house floor plan.

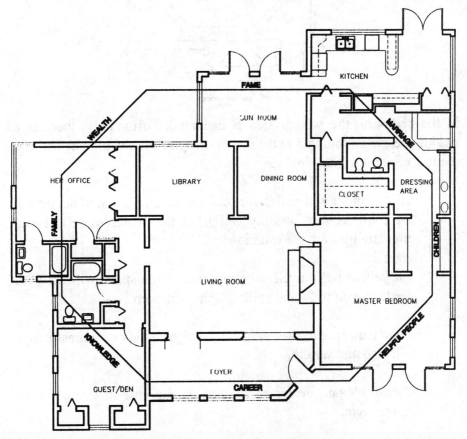

What could be done in the marriage area of this house? How about "his and her" monogrammed towels? Are they in one of the colors representative of marriage? Does the color coordinate with the rest of the bathroom?

What could be done to enhance wealth opportunities in the primary and secondary rooms?

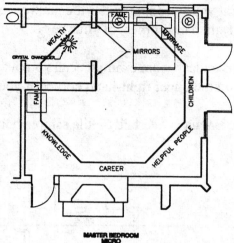

In the bedroom, the wealth area is excluded. Fortunately, there is a wealth-energizing fountain in the courtyard. (See the site plan in *The Site* section.) Solutions may include:

> Mirrors or art with reflective surfaces hung adjacent to the *wealth area* will enable wealthy Chi from the Water to reflect and circulate through the room.

> Put yellow bulb in the dressing area so the space will fill with wealthy *gold* light and spill into the bedroom.

> *Metal* hardware drawer pulls on the night stands with brass lamps will also add wealth..

> Use an elegant design style such as Baroque or another rich, ornate style.

> Add too many pillows (signifying that you have all that you need and more) in satin or other *expensive* [21] fabrics.

---

[21] A few well-placed accessories will dress an ordinary environment. In the example, fancy pillows will make an inexpensive bedspread more impressive.

Cotton chintz is expensive-looking and reasonably priced.

Design with rich colors such as gold, silver, purple and reds.

Add gold braid trim on the bedspread or window treatments.

In the secondary room for enhancement:

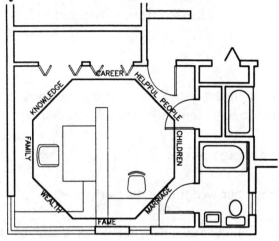

HER OFFICE
MICRO

It would be wise to put a mirror on the back of the bathroom door to encourage Chi to circulate. Additionally, Chi would bounce off the mirror, so wealth would not go into the bathroom.

In the wealth area of the office, accessorize with items representative (to you) of wealthy things. In a metal frame, hang a real or faux one hundred dollar bill, and paste your face on top of Mr. Franklin's. A fun project and solution could be to hang a piece of purple[22] poster board in the wealth area. Every time you encounter a wealthy situation, such as finding a lucky penny on the street or landing a new account, have a ceremony and paste a coin[23] on the board. You will create your own wealth-generating experience and *wealth-enhancing art.*

---

[22] Blue, purple, and red are representative of wealth; please refer to Bagua wheel.

[23] Coins represent and are representative of the Metal element. Be careful not to accessorize with too much *Metal,* which could offset the elemental balance.

Got the idea? It is said you need money to make money. You don't have to spend a lot; just be wise in how you set priorities. Act like you have plenty!

Believe and trust that the universe is full of effortless abundance!

Use your own creativity for other solutions in the additional life situation areas. Here are some more ideas to get you started:

In the marriage area:

Hang your wedding picture or white lace gloves.

Put wedding mementos or gifts on a table in the Marriage Gua.

Get a four-poster bed and drape it with white lace.

Dress the bed with red silk sheets.

Fill a champagne bucket with delicate white and pink fresh or silk flowers.

Don't forget to set the intent with the 4 C's of marriage:

Commitment, Communication, Cultivation, and Compromise!

In the children area:

Whether you have or would like to have children, a better relationship with them, or simply to honor the child within you:

> Put your teddy bear or special stuffed animal in the area.
> *(You DO still have it, don't you?)*

> If you don't have a special stuffed animal, go get one. Have a great time picking out the perfect one.

> Buy a baby accessory, like an antique basket, and use it as a pot for dried baby's breath and other flowers.

In the fame area:

> Hang a favorite picture of yourself in a red frame.

> Have you seen the mirror with the overlay of *Time* or *Newsweek*? Get one and hang it so your face is reflected as you pass by.

In the helpful people/travel area:

> Take a photography class so you can put up pictures from your own travel experiences.

> Place or hang objects representing places you have been or places you would like to go.

> Hang art of people smiling and having fun.

In the career area:

> Select items that represent the career that you have, would like to have, or that you want to be more fulfilling.

An attorney might like to use an unusual scale (scales of justice) as an accessory. A nautical architect might have famous ship blueprints framed and hung.

In the knowledge/self-cultivation area:

Get a comfortable lounge chair with a good light, and use it for reading and meditation.

Put books that you want to read in the area where you can see them.

Put up inspirational posters, or frame your favorite quotes.

You may also want to try to incorporate the auspicious Bagua shape in your designs; examples may include:

The selection of such furniture as a table or a modular sofa unit designed in that shape.

The layout of your furniture (This works functionally well in such seating arrangements as a living or family room.)

Millwork designs in the ceiling or paneling.

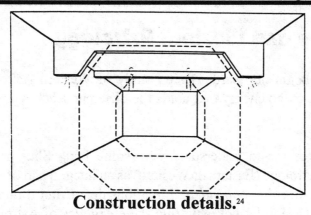

Construction details.[24]

Accessorize with Bagua-shaped items such as mirrors or picture frames. (I have a drum in the Bagua shape hanging on the wall.)

You can even eat from octagon-shaped plates and drink auspicious liquid in octagon vessels.

The essence of Feng Shui as Earth Design is to surround yourself with *life accessories* that are energetically representative for you. How do you feel when you are surrounded by all that you desire?

Surround yourself in what you already are!

Proceed with your Earth Design project as you would to attain all of your other goals with:

Intent, Dedication, Desire, Purposeful
and Loving Persistence!

---

[24] The traditional and much less expensive solution is to hang Chinese bamboo flutes to create the Bagua in three-dimensional volume. Flutes may also be hung in the life situation area that you would like to enhance. Make sure to hang the flutes at the proper angle represented by the appropriate side of the octagon.

What if a Chinese flute does not fit in with the harmony of your decor? When you understand the concept, your intuition will guide you to select a suitable alternative.

Chinese and Western Astrology

Before we begin our Earth Design study of Western Astrology, let's briefly look at the energy that holds the different schools of geomancy together.

It is hard for me to understand why some Feng Shui practitioners disregard Astrology (Eastern or Western) as an integral part of geomancy. With all the exciting *coincidental* relationships, I find it impossible to limit Earth Design by not exploring the energetics of Astrology. Both Western and Eastern Astrology are represented extensively through historical geomancy and are validated by scientific principles of magnetics.

From Hermetic tradition, *As above, So below*, clearly defines the sacred relationship of the ancient earth people to heaven and earth. The Chinese were no different. Chinese astronomers, astrologers, and geographers identified the dragons, tigers, tortoise, and phoenix of the classic site landscape configuration in correlation with the shapes and directions they observed in the constellations.

Master Ni is the living heir to the wisdom transmitted through an unbroken succession of seventy-four generations of Taoist Masters. In his interpretation of the *I Ching*, he devotes an entire chapter, called *Spiritual Implication of the Sky*, that details Eastern Astrology through traditional Chinese thought.

He writes, "The universe is the first expression of primal Chi."[b] He describes the relationships of heavenly bodies directly to the Bagua and Trigrams. As you recall, the Trigrams, among other things, define physical, directional, elemental, and life situations.

Master Ni even provides charts[c] that illustrate the relationship between Western and Eastern astrological phases (including the Western astrological *signs*). He connects the days of the week (using Western and Eastern astrological *planets*). This information further confirms how astrological theory was incorporated in Chinese philosophy.

seven day cycle	corresponding heavenly bodies	five elementary phases of a day
Thursday	Jupiter	growing day of wood
Friday	Venus	rigid day of metal
Saturday	Saturn	reposeful day of earth (elementary)
Sunday	Sun	brilliant day of sun
Monday	Moon	shimmering day of moon
Tuesday	Mars	consuming day of fire
Wednesday	Mercury	moving day of water

Similarities of Yearly Cyclic Phases and Western Terms

子 (Tze)	Aquarius	午 (Wu)	Leo
丑 (Chui)	Capricorn	未 (Wei)	Cancer
寅 (Ein)	Sagittarius	申 (Shen)	Gemini
卯 (Mao)	Scorpio	酉 (Yu)	Taurus
辰 (Chen)	Libra	戌 (Shu)	Aries
巳 (Sze)	Virgo	亥 (Hai)	Pisces

The *I Ching,* through the discussion of the *Celestial* Stems and the *Terrestrial* Branches, defines the workings of the heaven and earth relationship. It identifies that the direction and quality of Chi is different every two hours. *Coincidentally*, from a Western astrological perspective, the two-hour block is what determines a person's rising sign, based upon his/her time of birth.

Even without understanding the complexities of the *I Ching*, Eastern/Western astrology, or earth magnetic science, consider the Yin-Yang wheel. *How can heaven exist without earth? What is the life force that holds the two together?*

Astrology and Magnetics

During the continuous development of Feng Shui (early Han Dynasty, 206 BC-220 AD), due to the solar shift, magnetic north was in direct alignment to Polaris, also known as the North or Emperor Star. Heaven was organized according to the natural laws within physical space. "Everything terrestrial has its prototype, its primordial cause, and its ruling agency in heaven, and the influence on the stars and cosmic process on earth is geomancy's main concern." [d]

The Chinese recognize that the planets *Jupiter* and *Saturn* (my favorites) greatly affect the patterns of the magnetic fields on earth, causing subtle magnetic shifts. Through astrological and geomantic observation, Jupiter and Saturn *conjunct,* or come together and begin a new cycle, every 20 years. This conjunction causes a major shift in the earth's magnetic pattern, thus changing the energetic dynamic.

In the book, *Cycles of Becoming: The Planetary Pattern of Growth,* Alexander Ruperti defines the 20-year Jupiter/Saturn cycle as the "development of social destiny." During the conjunction,[25] "Saturn consolidates and makes concrete the type and quality of social participation envisioned by Jupiter." [e]

By jumping a bit into the next chapter, we can make a disciplined (Saturn) new start of living up to our abundant (Jupiter) vision of greater health, wealth, and happiness through utilizing the magnetic and planetary energies.

Let's take abundantly-full advantage of the sacred geomantic connection of heaven and earth through Western Astrology and let's learn more about Astrology as Earth Design.

---

[25] There is a new cycle that starts every new moon. Do not think you have to wait 20 years to make a new start!

"Om Ma Ni Pad Me Hum"[26]

*"God I am One with Nature,
Nature I am One with God."*

This *mantra* is from Tantric Buddhism and is said by traditional Black Hat practitioners to strengthen and set Feng Shui cures.

The compassion mantra adds the mystical ingredients of body, mind, and speech to a Feng Shui cure.

Body: Hold your hands together as if you were praying.

Mind: Visualize the intent while speaking, and then let it go.

Speech: Say the mantra nine times.

You were just given a sacred Feng Shui cure and gift. With such a gift, Professor Lin Yun, the Master of the Black Hat Sect suggests we follow the *tradition of the red envelope,* as I did when I received this information.

When a mystical Feng Shui cure is shared from one person to another, it is important that the receiver give a red envelope with something of value inside back to the giver. This exchange honors the work received, sets the intent, and protects the giver from any negative energy.

Should you use this cure or share it with someone else, please honor the red envelope, and advise them of the tradition.

---

[26] Please refer to "D-OM-e is H-OM-e," Chapter 3, *Natural Science*, and "Setting the Intent," Chapter 4, *Intuition*.

"When one is harmoniously positioned in the universe, both balance and harmony will bless one's life: when one is in flow with the powerful workings of nature and the cosmos, one's health, prosperity, and mental state will benefit."

Sarah Rossbach [a]

Astrology

What is your sign? We have all been asked that question and probably read our horoscope in the local paper. Admit it! Astrology is not such a mystery.

The ancients started practicing Astrology[1] by recognizing cycles of cosmic natural law. By observing the heavens, early astrologers could predict changing seasons and prepare themselves by finding shelter for the winter or beginning to plant crops in the spring. When they recognized different heavenly clusters, the ancients started to connect the dots to make pictures. The images of a goat (Capricorn) or a lion (Leo), for example, became part of their mythology. As observation continued, the ancients recognized energetic characteristics according to the positioning of heavenly bodies.

---

[1] All of the principles in this chapter are based upon Western Astrology; Chinese Astrology is a different system.

Astrology became part of their mythology and spirituality, influencing their way of life, and accordingly, the design of their buildings (as briefly discussed in Chapter 2).

While using Astrology in your Earth Design project is not necessary, I highly recommend it because the relationships of the heavenly bodies are integral to the harmonics of the earth's natural laws. Science has confirmed how different phases of the moon magnetically influence the earth's gravitational forces, including all bodies of water. We know both scientifically and intuitively that our human body, which is comprised of over 90% water, is also affected.

Science validates that moon phases affect the tension of our skin. Psychological studies have verified that there is more *lunatic-like* (luna means of the moon) behavior during the time of the full moon.[2] Even *PMS (Pre-Menstrual Syndrome)* ties into the Astrological and life cycle. PMS is a physical manifestation of the moon's gravitational pull. When a woman is *on her moon,*[3] her fluids are different from the way they are during the other times of month. Gravity affects a shift in the waters, which directly influences her emotions and personality.

As with many earth societies, Native Americans respected *moon time* as a joining of our humanness with the earth. This concept comes directly from one of the most sacred Native American prayers: *All comes from Woman.* **Mother Earth?** Perhaps the physical and physiological effects are meant to be felt on a regular basis in order to experience this sacred connection.

In newspaper Astrology, we are most familiar with our *Sun Sign,* which is the location of the sun at the time we were born. However, all of the planets were in the sky, in a specific location, at the precise moment of our birth. Therefore, according to natural law and astrological principles,

---

[2] On a monthly basis, the moon cycle waxes and wanes from new to full to new. (It is interesting to note that there are 8 cycles, just like the life situations of the Bagua wheel.) All the planets have relationships to each other in the same way that the earth has a relationship with the moon. When we are sensitive, we can also experience the phases of these planetary relationships.

[3] Moon is the Native American's term for menstruation.

all the energies of the heavenly bodies and gravitational forces have an effect on us.

Astrology as Earth Design is the study of the combined planetary energies, which is as personal and individual as fingerprints. All the planets, by their qualities and energies, influence our lives; however, even two people who were born at the same moment have different Astrological charts.[4] Planet locations are oriented from the place of birth; therefore, magnetic and gravitational forces affect them differently.

I am not an Astrologer, and I have only a very basic understanding of the subject. *Real Astrologers* have an amazing understanding of the planetary energies that guide us in unlimited possibilities. They can provide very personal information about the *circles inside circles*[5] or the many levels of interplay between the planets, signs, and houses. There is an abundance of life information that they can assess through the *natal chart*[6] at the time of your birth and the ever changing multi-dimensional planetary relationships.

If you use basic Astrology principles, you can add another dimension to your Earth Design project, further aligning your personal planetary energy to your supportive environment. Using the energies of the planets further connects you to the natural harmonics and increases your maximum potential.

Using *baking a cake* as an analogy, when you combine all the ingredients in the proper proportions you have the potential for delicious perfection. Baking, however, requires patience and some experience. You may have

---

[4]   An Astrological chart is the way the planet positions in the sky are graphically represented.

[5]   Our astrological chart is our very own life story mandala.

[6]   I recommend that you have your natal and local space chart available while you are reading this chapter.

to *bake your Astrology as Earth Design cake* a few times. Astrology[7] is a life study. I have tried my best to simplify the basics so you can use the planetary energies to enhance your well-being. As you go through the chapter, I promise that if you take your time and go step by step, you will be rewarded.

Astrology can give you valuable information about your life. Here is my story . . .

> For the longest time, I had been resistant to learning Astrology because of my own skepticism. From what little I did remember from a class I had taken, I did not feel the energy.
>
> After being exposed to people I respected who understood Astrology, I took another class. By gaining more knowledge, I began to appreciate my astrological *life circle*. I began to understand astrology from looking at past events that were clearly symbolized in my chart.
>
> Because of **Transiting[8] Saturn[9] hitting (crossing over) my natal Saturn in 1985**, I understood why I had been so driven to make my design business successful. The intensity of this focus lasted for about eight years because Transiting Saturn was not scheduled to hit another planet until January, 1994.

---

[7] This is not a text on Astrology, only basic aspects applicable to Earth Design will be discussed. Should Astrology interest you further, I recommend that you read about it more completely. The more you know, the greater understanding you will have regarding your life purpose.

[8] As a transiting planet gets closer to a planet in the natal chart, the energy of the first planet is felt progressively less, and the next planet is felt progressively more.

[9] Saturn is representative of the task-master, discipline, and order.

But in 1993, my old way of practicing design was not fun anymore. In Retrospect, I recognized **Transiting Saturn** (discipline and order) **was getting closer to my Natal Mars** (drive, creative initiative) **in Aquarius** (humanitarian, spiritual) **in the 9th House** (higher-minded philosophy, publishing). Publishing?

> *Was I to focus on my planetary purpose to have fun again? What was Saturn, the taskmaster planet, suggesting that I do to be happy and grow according to my contract?*[10]

> *The planets suggested that I take intuitive and innovative action for humanitarian and spiritual social change.* What a task!

I saw Venus (beauty, security) **and Uranus** (instincts, originality, mass consciousness) **in Cancer** (nurturing, security, home) **in my 2nd House** (self esteem, natural talent).

> *I had to give and receive nurturing through beauty in the home (or office) environment. I could liberate myself by instinctively sharing my natural talent for design.*

I saw Pluto (drive for self mastery, transformation) **conjunct** (blended with) **Jupiter** (expansion, opportunity) **in Leo** (exciting, creative) **in my 3rd House** (communication, clarity) .

> *My search for expanded meaning helped me realize my destiny was to transform the collective through creative expression and communication.*

I saw Neptune (transcendence, spiritual duty) **in Libra** (search for balance) **in my 5th House** (risk, creativity).

---

[10] The *contract* is the karmic arrangement or mission in life that is made between an individual and the universe. The time and place of birth is in accordance with the karmic contract. The reason that astrological charts have such great significance is because they help define our personal Chi.

I recognized that I had the capacity to be fulfilled by transcending myself through creative projects and risk taking. "If I surrender to my destiny, I will create harmony and balance for myself by sharing it with others."

Gemini (communication: writing, teaching and speaking) **Sun, Taurus** (the earth sign of home, beauty & stability) **rising**.

While creatively exploring the potential of Earth Design, through astrological confirmation, I realized that I was Earth Design and Earth Design was me. As I continued to learn more Astrology, it continued to validate my instincts. I was on my true spiritual path.

Through my communication abilities, it was my destiny to share Earth Design with you in order to grow. Earth Design is confirmation of my Astrological story at this period in my life.

*Now, let's apply this valuable tool to **your** Earth Design project*

Astrology and Color

By studying an astrological chart, you discover color schemes that are aligned with your color vibration. When using appropriate colors, you feel at home, as if your environment were a second skin.

Because there are inconsistencies between sources due to the interpretive nature of the art, I will not present the traditional astrological color representations or give many examples. Because Earth Design as Astrology is an intuitive practice and personal to you, it is best to develop color representations that personally feel right. In addition, examples I may provide could alter or influence your decisions. When your colors *feel* right, they *are* right.

I have found that people that have definite color preferences intuitively know the colors that personally feel right on all levels. Interestingly, it is typical that they subconsciously select either their dominant chart colors or the colors represented by the energy of missing voids in their life situations.[11]

Whether or not you have color favorites, if you do the exercises from an intuitive and feeling perspective instead of from association or intellectual representation, when you look at your chart through your selected colors, the right astrological color scheme will develop for you. You can do it.

Allow this information to come through you!

You are your greatest asset!

The Signs

The zodiac wheel is segmented into twelve different sections called *signs*. The signs are the first sheet of your overlay.

When you are learning Astrology, it is easiest to look at a chart from the beginning of a *New Year*. The traditional New Year begins on March 21st with the birth of spring (the time of the vernal equinox). Consider the dawn of a new day; the sun rises in the east, and the *dawn of a new year* is shown on the east side of a chart.

As you probably know from newspaper Astrology, Aries is the first sign of the New Year. As the year progresses, the signs change about every thirty days. They move from east to west (sunrise to sunset)[12] and back again, just like the Yin-Yang life circle.

---

[11] Because your chart is an ever-changing life cycle, your color representations may change as you do. Life experiences also explains why tastes change and develop.

[12] Either the symbols of the signs or an abbreviation will be on your computer-generated chart.

The signs in progression are:

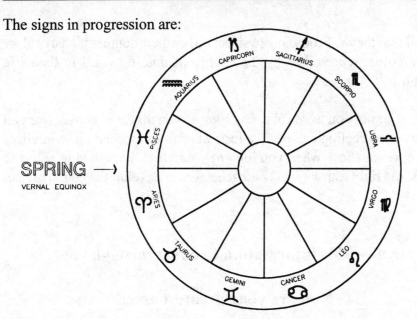

SPRING ⟶
VERNAL EQUINOX

Exercise: *In a quiet place, set the intent. "I am going to read the characteristics of the signs, and the color that feels right to me will enter my mind's eye quickly." Write the color down in the "color" blank. (Feel free to make copies of the sign and planet pages to make them easy to use when you are working with your natal and local space charts.)*

Please leave the "Full Color Description" blank until the next exercise.

Key Words for the Signs:

Aries: (Fire/Cardinal) assertive, brave, first, energetic, self-oriented, self-confident, impulsive competitive, pioneering, spontaneous, active, self-confident, takes initiative, creative, "infants of the zodiac"

Color: _____

Full Color Description: _____

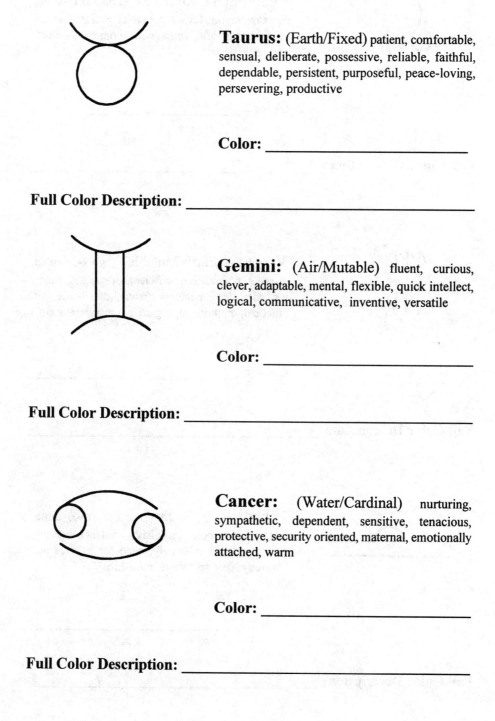

Taurus: (Earth/Fixed) patient, comfortable, sensual, deliberate, possessive, reliable, faithful, dependable, persistent, purposeful, peace-loving, persevering, productive

Color: _____

Full Color Description: _____

Gemini: (Air/Mutable) fluent, curious, clever, adaptable, mental, flexible, quick intellect, logical, communicative, inventive, versatile

Color: _____

Full Color Description: _____

Cancer: (Water/Cardinal) nurturing, sympathetic, dependent, sensitive, tenacious, protective, security oriented, maternal, emotionally attached, warm

Color: _____

Full Color Description: _____

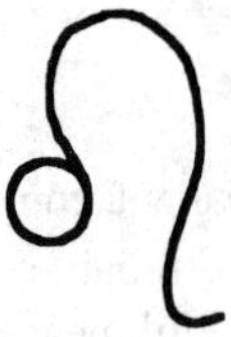

Leo: (Fire/Fixed) creative, honest, risk-taking, charismatic, fun-loving, generous, exciting, warm-hearted, dramatic, courageous, commands attention, affectionate

Color: _____

Full Color Description: _____

Virgo: (Earth/Mutable) work-oriented, discreet, painstaking, efficient, pragmatic, exacting, articulate, neatness freaks, detail-oriented, practical, methodical, organized, discriminating

Color: _____

Full Color Description: _____

Libra: (Air/Cardinal) cooperative, diplomatic, courteous, indecisive, balance-seeking, contrary, lover of beauty, need for balance and harmony, face-to-face relationships

Color: _____

Full Color Description: _____

Scorpio: (Water/Fixed) penetrating, secretive, resourceful, compulsive, scientific, obsessive, intense, manipulating, regenerative, powerful, investigative, physiological

Color: _____

Full Color Description: _____

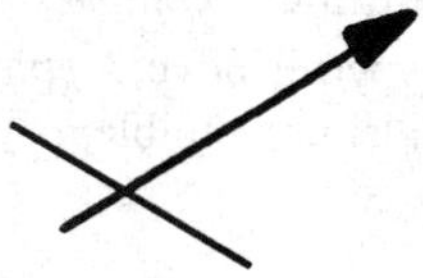

Sagittarius: (Fire/Mutable) benevolent, optimistic, extravagant, high- minded, enthusiastic, idealistic, expansive, impulsive, intuitive, patient, encouraging

Color: _____

Full Color Description: _____

Capricorn: (Earth/Cardinal) responsible, traditional, authoritative, achievement and career oriented, wants public recognition, concern with social status, ambitious, organized

Color: _____

Full Color Description: _____

Aquarius: (Air/Fixed) objective, rebellious, futuristic, independent, eccentric, inventive, humanitarian, universal, progressive, experimentive, unique

Color: _____

Full Color Description: _____

Pisces: (Water/Mutable) compassionate, mystical, illusory, hypersensitive, spiritual, dreamy, idealistic, considerate, humble, psychic, inspirational

Color: _____

Full Color Description: _____

Exercise: *Next to the sign descriptions, the **Astrological Element** and the **Quality** of each sign is presented. Using the element and quality definitions, review the colors that you determined and define them further. Write a specific full color description. You may have already instinctively added the nature of the color through its elements and quality.*

Determine the degree of lightness, darkness, brightness or dullness of the sign colors. Using red as an example, is the color a pastel pink, like a baby bonnet? Does it have neutral qualities like rust? Is it a jewel color, like ruby, or is it a muddy red like dusty rose or terracotta? Is the blue the color of a clear spring day fully illuminated with the sun, rich with green/black, like the depths of the ocean, or a deep and full-bodied blue/violet color after the sun sets? Try to be as specific as you can, it will help when selecting textiles, textures, and paint in Chapter 7.

Color has no limitation.

The Elements of the Signs

Fire: enthusiastic, energetic, impulsive, spontaneous, intense, stimulating, creative, impulsive, optimistic, independent

Earth: practical, materialistic, down-to-earth, realistic, security minded, productive, methodical, exacting, orderly, patient

Air: intellectual, questioning, conceptualizing, synthesizing, observant, objective, interacting, cooperative

Water: moody, sensitive, responsive, nurturing, intuitive, imaginative, flowing, dependent, vulnerable, sympathetic

The Qualities of the Signs

Cardinal: active, restless, energetic, driving, ambitious, takes initiative

Fixed: determined, purposeful, persistent, stubborn, inflexible

Mutable: adaptable, varietal, changeable, personal, serving, introspective

The positions of the planets are overlaid on the sign chart. Visualize it this way: The heavens are divided into the twelve signs, through which the ten[13] traditional planets are continuously traveling.

Each planet has a direct relationship to the signs,[14] called *rulership*. Rulership is another way of describing similar energies. For example:

The planet **Mars**

Rules

The planet **Aries**

because of the similar qualities.

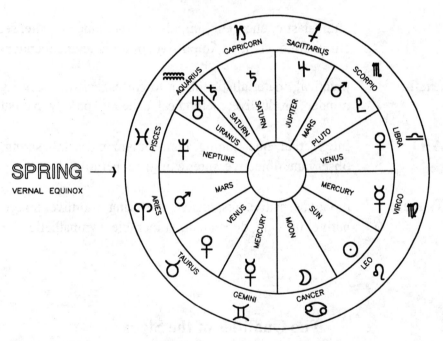

<hr />

[13]   These are the nine traditional planets plus the moon.

[14]   The traditional astrological exceptions seen in the graphic are as follows:

Scorpio is ruled by both Mars and Pluto. Pluto is the higher octave of Mars. This means Pluto has the same energetics, but with more spiritual depth.

The first half of Aquarius is ruled by Saturn and the last half by Uranus. Aquarius asks that we do the work to become enlightened.

Exercise: *Go back to your quiet place, read through the character-istics of each planet, and write down your intuitive color representation. Look at the planet/sign wheel to see if there is color similarity between the sign and the ruling planet.*

Before moving on to the next planet, visualize yourself in a room with the walls and ceiling painted in your selected color. Fill the room with people that have the attributes of the sign and ruler. Write down the energy that you experience. This part of the exercise will help you to feel the planetary energies in your environment when you get to the local space section.

Example: When I consider the characteristics of the planet Mars and the sign Aries, I create a Red room in my mind's eye (remember, your color may be different), and I fill it with people who are aggressive and innovative. The energy that I feel is electric, active, and in fast forward.

Key Words for the Planets

Sun: (Fire) self esteem, life force, vitality, creativity, risk-taking, charisma, spirituality, individuality, the root of who you are, ego, soul's task, planet of life and spiritual essence

Color:_____

Energy/Feeling: _____

Moon: (Water) emotions, security, caretaking instincts, nurturing, moody, instinctive, receptive, feelings, love, sensitivities, maternal, vulnerabilities, planet of fertility

Color:_____

Energy/Feeling: _____

Mercury: (Air) communication, thinking, adaptability, clarity, information, intellect, rational, logic, perception, gathering skills, planet of reason

Color:_____

Energy/Feeling: _____

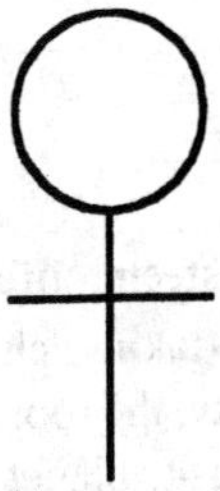

Venus: (Earth) desire for pleasure, sensuality, urge for comfort and ease through financial security, consistent, thoughtful, tangible beauty, planet of love

Color:_____

Energy/Feeling: _____

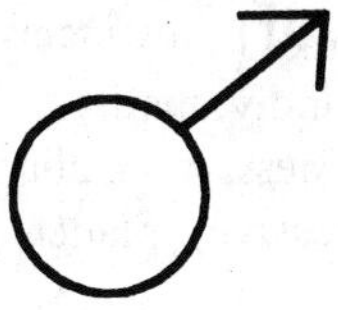

Mars: (Fire) assertion, drive, independence, personal power, challenging, spontaneous instincts, willful directness, self expression, confident, determined, planet of action

Color:_____

Energy/Feeling: _____

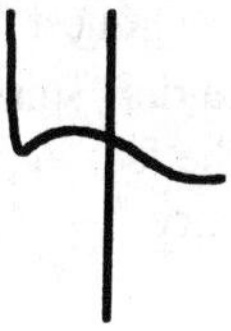

Jupiter: (Fire) ideals and goals, optimism, quest for truth, expansion, highest expectations, seeking the best, abundance, opportunity, grace, planet of expansion

Color:_____

Energy/Feeling: _____

Saturn: (Earth) practicality, status, effort, career, drives, teacher, ambitions, taskmaster, responsibility, lesson of physical incarnation, planet of discipline and focus

Color:_____

Energy/Feeling: _____

Uranus: (Air) instincts, higher-mindedness, individuality, freedom drives, inventiveness, originality, humanitarian, progressive, planet of mass consciousness

Color:_____

Energy/Feeling: _____

Neptune: (Water) quest for infinite love and beauty, intuition, spiritual duty, inspirational, aesthetic appreciation, planet of transcendence

Color:_____

Energy/Feeling: _____

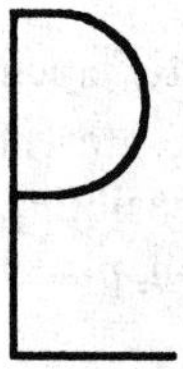

Pluto: (Water) intensity, drive for self mastery, probing, compulsions, eternalness, unity of organization, power of the soul, planet of regeneration and transformation

Color:_____

Energy/Feeling: _____

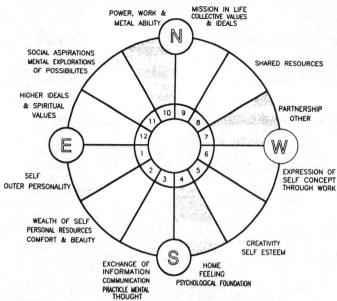

The numbered areas in the center wheel indicate the different areas of life, called *houses*. Houses represent *life situations*, similar to the Bagua. While all of the houses have significance, we will focus most of our attention on the most powerful houses on the cusps of the cardinal directions,[15] indicated by E (east), S (south), W (west), and N (north).

These houses define the polarities of our inner and outer selves, including:

1st House   Self and Outer Personality

4th House   Feelings and Home: Physical Body and Environment as Primary and Secondary Vessels

7th House   Partnership: With Self and Others

10th House Power, Work, and Mental Abilities.

Exercise: *Using your sign and planet color charts, determine your color scheme by filing in the blanks.*

---

[15]   Do you remember the power of the directions in the previous chapter?

1st House: What is the sign: _____/Color_____

Ruling planet of the sign: _____/Color_____

List the planets in the sign: _____/Color_____

_____/Color_____

_____/Color_____

_____/Color_____

4th House: What is the sign: _____/Color_____

Ruling planet of the sign: _____/Color_____

List the planets in the sign: _____/Color_____

_____/Color_____

_____/Color_____

_____/Color_____

7th House: What is the sign: _____/Color_____

Ruling planet of the sign: _____/Color_____

List the planets in the sign: _____/Color_____

_____/Color_____

_____/Color_____

_____/Color_____

10th House: What is the sign: _____/Color_____

Ruling planet of the sign: _____/Color_____

List the planets in the sign: _____/Color_____

_____/Color_____

_____/Color_____

_____/Color_____

In what Sign is your Sun: _____/Color_____

The predominate three colors are your   Color:_____
     Astrological Colors[16]

Color:_____

Color:_____

It should have been easy to determine the three dominant colors because they usually repeat themselves. As in most examples, the same color(s) keep revealing themselves as you work your way around the chart. Because an astrological chart is a blue print for confirming your life's purpose, the same information (and colors) repeat.

A chart is no different than a personal life experience. When you are paying attention to your life process, you will begin to notice different situations keep happening that try to teach you the same thing.

---

[16] Use these colors when determining the color scheme for your home and/or office. To help you, refer to the color section in *Conventional Interior Design*, Chapter 7.

I have been having terrible problems with my computers. I have lost so much time and information. There have been times they have been down for weeks. I get so frustrated.

The lesson: I have no control over some situations, so I need to trust that everything happens in its own perfect time, to be patient with life and myself, and to be grateful for the opportunity to give myself some off time.

I got it! But please don't crash again. I'll freak. Did I really get it?

It is your contract! If you don't get it one way, it will come at you in another until you take notice and begin to learn. By surrounding yourself with the appropriate colors, your personal Chi will grow, and all aspects of your life will be enhanced.

**Surrender to your life purpose.
It is a requirement for happiness!**

The Local Space Overlay

Earth Design also incorporates Astrology by overlaying an individual's local space chart in the center of a house or office floor plan. The local space chart has the same birth information as the natal chart with a few differences.

1.   A natal chart (with the east on the left side) is oriented with north at the bottom. The local space chart is oriented with north at the top of the chart.

2.   The natal chart is positioned from the longitude and latitude of the birth place. The local space chart is positioned from the longitude and latitude of the selected city. The *birth time* used in the local space chart is the same as the natal birth time adjusted to the location time zone.

3.   Only energies of the planets are used in a local space chart.

When a local space chart is oriented to the north as overlaid on a home or office floor plan, a great deal of personal information can be observed. In our environments, we make best use of planet representations to create personal energetic pathways.[17]

When using planet information, you align yourself with the specific planetary energies, thereby maximizing their energetic opportunities.

You superimpose the planets on top of your house to evaluate the influence of planetary energetics. Place the center of your transparent local space overlay in the center of your floor plan. Then, as shown, extend the *planet lines* from the center[18] of the home to each of the planets in both directions.

---

[17] These are personal ley lines.

Local space Astrology may also be used on a city map. By placing a local space chart at city hall, or the city center, the best personally energetic areas can be determined. Before choosing an area, you need to determine what you would like to accomplish while living in that city. If you are in your productive years, perhaps the best place to live is on the Mars (action) or Jupiter (expansion) line. If you are retired, perhaps Venus (beauty and grace) is more appropriate.

Additionally, by placing the local space chart on your selected location, you can decide the best lines to select a bank (Jupiter), children's school (Saturn), grocery store (Moon) or office (Sun/Mars).

[18] To find the center, either locate it by eye, use an architects' scale to measure, or try this trick. Cut the floor plan out, and fold it into equal quarters. When the plan is opened, the center point will be indicated by the crossing crease lines.

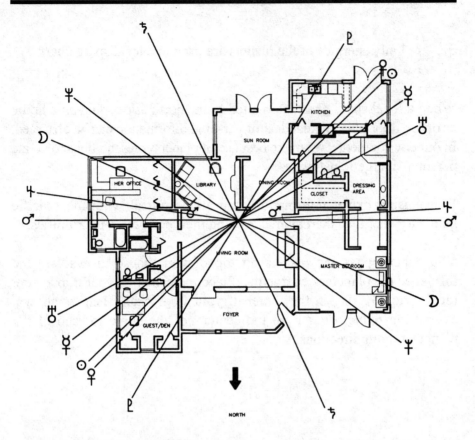

Using the intuitive information[19] gathered in the exercise when you surrounded yourself with people having the characteristics of the planets in the rooms painted with the planet colors, you can determine how the energy affects the lines in your home.

For example: In the room painted with the color of the sun, did the charismatic people full of creative individuality help you to feel vital and alive? Does it make sense to:

Sun: Locate areas of importance, and feature special items that define who you are.

---

[19] Refer to the Energy/Feeling blanks you filled in the last section.

How can you best use the energies? What *Elements* of the planets are represented? Consider the possibilities for both function and aesthetics.

> This area can be used to support you on all levels. Brightly illuminate (Fire) this area with an appropriate lighting fixture or sky light. This is a great area for entertaining and sharing yourself with others.

Moon: Locate areas for living things. This is a good area for a nursery or a kitchen where the family is nourished. This would probably not be a good work area because the energy may cause emotional sensitivity, perhaps creating tendencies for mood swings and vulnerabilities. As with all water planets, these lines show where water is present, including leaks.

Mercury: This line is perfect for all types of communication, study, and work areas for intellectual creativity. It is a great place for the family library or office.

Venus: This area is good for a master bedroom and places of tenderness. If there is a musician in the house, it is perfect for the music room. Place objects of beauty, artistry, or objects representative of what you desire. (Remember to set the intent.)

Mars: This area is great for an office or a major corridor to quickly get from one area to another. Be careful of all those sharp objects if Mars is in the kitchen. Too much fire could also cause you to get burned.[20] A Mars line will probably be too active to get restful sleep if it should cross the bed line.

---

[20] Perhaps you can use Water element objects and color to soften the sharp-angled metal knives, as in the destructive order described in *Feng Shui*, Chapter 5.

Jupiter: This line is typically the easiest and most generous spot. It is a good place for a family or living area because it encourages enjoyment, protection, and wealth. It is also a perfect area for a hidden safe.

Saturn: This area will generate the greatest focus, discipline, and stability. It is perfect for an office or for where the children do their homework.

Uranus: Do something out of the ordinary. Find playful or whimsical accents or furniture. Show your individuality, or create excitement in this area to promote excitement in your life. Do you have an unusual hobby? Can you do it there? You can hang pictures of your skydiving experiences. This line will probably be too erratic to relax in. Watch for loose wiring, extensive electromagnetic leakage, and electrical problems.

Neptune: This is a good area for personal reflection, growth, and appreciation. Be careful not to place an area that requires clarity (such as an office) here. Perceptions may be falsely altered. When on the Neptune line, secure all medicine chests and poisonous household substances from children to prevent accidental ingestion.

Pluto: This line is ideal for a bedroom; try to have it cross the bed, for healthy revitalizing rest. Objects appear new and bright, and you can always look for misplaced objects along this line.

Use the following explanation, the floor plan with the local space overlay (located several pages previously), planetary representations, and your energy/feeling descriptions to help with your evaluation:

Because the Sun (self-esteem, individuality, creativity, risk taking), Venus (the location to earn financial security), and Mercury (logic, thinking and communication), are in the North/East room, this space is the most appropriate room for an office.

Where should the Master bedroom be? Notice that the Moon (emotions, security, and feelings) crosses the bed. Nice.

Notice how the Moon (femininity) is in her office and her desk position. This is her place of control. Her active Mars line keeps (Moon) sensitivity high but leaves her no time to be emotional. She makes best use of the Jupiter (expansion) line where promotional materials are created, invoices are printed, and checks are deposited.

On the other side of the Jupiter line, she keeps the personal checkbook.

The Mars line shows exactly where the East/West *traffic* corridor is in the house.

If there is still work or reading to be done after a hard day, where would be a good place to position a comfortable chair? Look at the Saturn (discipline and focus) line in the library. All Earth Design decisions must be appropriate to the task, so don't forget to have non-glare lighting.

Meditation and relaxation? Notice the Neptune (divinity, spiritual depth, and transcendence) line is also in the library. When lighting is placed on a dimmer, the mood of the space can be transformed into a place of serenity.

Watery Pluto crosses the kitchen sink and dishwasher.

There are always problems with the toilets on the Uranus line.

Accents to Remedy or Enhance

If there are problem areas or an area that you would like to enhance, you can make adjustments. Solutions are conceptually the same as those you have already learned. By placing accessories represented by symbols of the signs on the appropriate planetary line, you can modify the energies. You can strengthen the effectiveness of any Earth Design enhancement by also combining Feng Shui remedies.

Consider the symbol, ruling planetary energy, shape, color, element (Astrological and Feng Shui), and generative/degenerative cycles when selecting a remedy or enhancement. Notice that the following solutions are very cost effective.[21]

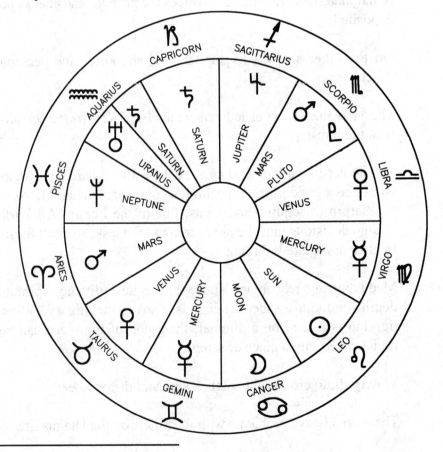

---

[21] Try to solve the condition by moving the function or furniture to a more appropriate location if it is architecturally feasible.

Sign:	Aries
Symbol:	Ram
Planet:	Mars
Astrology Element:	Fire
Feng Shui Element:[22]	Wood
Corresp. Planet/Element:[23]	Jupiter/Fire
Color:[24]	Red?/Green/Red
Shape/Quality/Element: [25]	Sharp Angles/Fire

Condition: A bed on the Mars line may be too active to get restful sleep, or you and your mate may always argue.

Ideas: Put out the fire. Add Earth and/or Water to modify the Fire by using flat or irregular-shaped details. How about a blue and green bed spread with a wavy line pattern?

---

[22] On the East side of the Bagua, the vernal equinox of the Astrology wheel was overlaid at the same point according to the ecliptic cycle of the seasonal variations of the twelve branches, defined in the *I Ching*. The Feng Shui element was determined by where the *Western* planet aligned with the elemental energetic of the Bagua.

[23] The *Feng Shui Planet* is according to the corresponding element of the Bagua.

The element listed after the *Feng Shui Planet* is the *Western Astrological Element* of the planet.

[24] The first color is only my representation for the Western Astrological representation. It is better to use the color you have determined. The second color is the *Feng Shui color* represented by the Bagua. The third is the representation of the Feng Shui color represented by the Astrological element.

[25] Because form takes precedence in Earth Design, the shape/quality is an intuitive blend of the above energetics with an Astrological slant. The intuitive element is based upon the generative and destructive cycles. In the case of Aries for example, Fire is dominant over Wood.

(Water is represented by the colors, form, and softness of the spread. It is a large enough item to put out the Fire.)

How about pottery table lamps with a flat shape in a neutral Earth color or stone tops on the night stand? What about painting an accent wall a cooling color and adding a Water coordinating wallcovering border? Using the Bagua, hang a soothing picture of a seascape in the health area.

Remember to consider the Feng Shui Horoscopes of the particular space and person. In this idea, if your natal sign is Water, for example, it is better to add more Earth to the room than to drown it in too much Water, which may make it difficult for you to get out of bed.

Condition: An office on the Neptune line produces too much deception and mystery, no focused action.

Ideas: Add the fire of Mars. Put a red triangle (Fire shape) at eye level, so it is visible when looking up from the desk. Then, forget it. It can be so subtle that your boss will not even notice. Look for a sculpture, a painting, or create your own, such as a ram on a steep red-rock mountain. Why can't the sculpture be placed in the career area of your desk?[26] Hang motivating art on the wall in the career area.

---

[26] Using the Bagua, you will notice the sculpture will be located in an impractical location. Instead, how about putting something red and fiery in the pencil drawer?

Sign:	Taurus
Symbol:	Bull
Planet:	Venus
Astrology Element:	Earth
Feng Shui Element:	Water
Corresp. Planet/Element:	----
Color:	Neutrals of Green, Olive, and Brown?
	Black, Blue and Green/Yellow
Shape/Quality/Element:	Flat shapes with soft detailing Water

Condition: Venus helps to define what makes you feel accomplished. This energy is auspicious in any area by adding grace to the activity of the area.

Ideas: Add a beautiful accent specific to the task of the space.

Sign:	Gemini
Symbol:	Twins
Planet:	Mercury
Astrology Element:	Air
Feng Shui Element:	Water
Corresp. Planet/Element:	Mercury/Air
Color:	Yellow?/Black/--
Shape/Quality/Element:	Straight-shaped, transparent objects Water and Air

Condition: Mercury works well in most areas. Perhaps you may want greater mind focus and intellect in an office or study area.

Ideas: Add such accents as a graphic of doors because the symbol of Gemini looks like a gate, which may be interesting and appropriate to hang in the career, wealth, or fame areas. Walk though the gate of your mind as you enter the office. Add Air or Water items, such as a live plant[27] growing in water in a clear glass vase, and watch the roots grow. Surround yourself with books that personally inspire you.

As previously discussed, a crystal ball overhead can also focus Chi inward.

Condition: With Mercury in the meditation or bedroom area, it may be difficult to turn off the thoughts in your head.

Ideas: Add the Water of Neptune and/or Uranus energy, slow down, and turn off. Allow the depth of the higher-minded planets to enter your empty mind. Add the depth and stillness of the ocean. Whatever the color scheme, determine an area that can be painted a deep (heat absorbing) color. Will deep blue or purple be a nice coordinate? If that idea is not appropriate, how about leaving all the lights off during meditation, except the lamp with a purple or blue light bulb?

---

[27] The plant will purify and refresh the air for greater clarity and absorb electromagnetic radiation from the equipment.

Sign:	Cancer
Symbol:	Crab
Planet:	Moon
Astrology Element:	Water
Feng Shui Element:	Water
Corresp. Planet/Element:	Mercury/Air
Color:	White, Silver?/Black/--
Shape/Quality/Element:	Soft curves and Concave shapes Water

Condition: The only place that the Moon line may be problematic is in the office. You may not be able to control your emotions here, which is undesirable in a professional environment. This condition may be volatile if it is combined with Water in either your natal chart or your Feng Shui horoscope.

Ideas: When Earth is added, Water is lessened (land fills oceans), and when Fire is added to Earth, more Earth is created. Fire will stimulate and focus the mind, while Earth will stabilize it. Add a flat yellow bar underneath the red triangle (similar to the Mars suggestion.)

Condition: To be sensitive and feeling is usually not a problem. It is the basis of expanded intuitive development, leading to spiritual cultivation and a more purposeful and gracious life.

Ideas: For greater sensitivity, find a crab carved out of black onyx stone (Earth) or a traditional stone scarab beetle (the Egyptian symbol of the Soul), and put it on a table in the self-cultivation area.

Sign:	Leo
Symbol:	Lion
Planet:	Sun
Astrology Element:	Fire
Feng Shui Element:	Metal
Corresp. Planet/Element:	----
Color:	Gold?/White, Black and Grey/Red
Shape/Quality/Element:	Round/Fire

Condition: The Sun line is auspicious in any area; it is your personal space.

Ideas: Add representations of this energy by determining areas in your life where you would like to add greater self esteem, creativity, and individuality. In your office, add Fire and Metal objects or colors in the appropriate areas.

Hang a *Lion King* movie poster or place a stuffed lion in your insecure child's bedroom in his self-cultivation area. Also, put a picture of yourselves in a red metal frame so he/she knows you are always there.

Sign:	Virgo
Symbol:	Maiden
Planet:	Mercury
Astrology Element:	Earth
Feng Shui Element:	Metal
Corresp. Planet/Element:	Venus/Earth

Color:	Neutral Browns and Yellows? White/Yellow[28]
Shape/Quality/Element:	Straight and Solid/Earth

Condition: When the Mercury line is in the office, it may misdirect mental energy. If there is a lot of Virgo in this person's chart, it is possible he will get hung up in the details and never see the forest through the trees.

Ideas: Buy an executive toy that has a magnetic base with the shaped metal pieces that create mini sculptures. (I've even seen the metal shape in a dollar sign; perfect.) If you realize that you are stuck in the details, playing with the metal toy will help focus your mind.

Instead of placing one overhead crystal (as you did for Gemini), hang four in a box (in nine-inch increments) with your head as the central point for inward focus.

---

[28] Yellow may be inappropriate in a design scheme. Consider burnt umber, burnt sienna, gold, or cream.

Sign:	Libra
Symbol:	Scales
Planet:	Venus
Astrology Element:	Air
Feng Shui Element:	Metal
Corresp. Planet/Element:	Venus/Earth
Color:	Dusty Pinks?
	White/--
Shape/Quality/Element:	Stable objects with soft lines/Earth

Condition: The Grace of Venus adds harmony and balance.

Ideas: Hang a diptych [29] (2) or tryptic (3), in a gold frame, in the Gua you would like to enhance. The individual pieces combined will form the balanced piece. Make sure you leave the appropriate two or three inches between them.

Sign:	Scorpio
Symbol:	Scorpion
Planet:	Pluto
Astrology Element:	Water
Feng Shui Element:	Fire
Corresp. Planet/Element:	----
Color:	Blackish Red?/Red, Pink and White/Black
Shape/Quality/Element:	Hidden Objects/Water

Condition: Be careful when Pluto lines fall exactly across furniture located and designed for a specific task: a bed, a chair, a desk, or a sofa. While you are in that place, you may

---

[29] Two or more pieces of art in a series that are all framed the same way.

receive information that has secret meanings or is misleading.

Ideas: The first and best solution is to recognize this problem and learn to discriminate.

Condition: Using Plutonian energy is great for healing and recharging your batteries.

Ideas: Add deep Water colors (aquas, blues and violets) and curvilinear shapes. The space should feel good. Chi should not move too fast or too slowly.

Sign:	Sagittarius
Symbol:	Centaur/Arrows
Planet:	Jupiter
Astrology Element:	Fire
Feng Shui Element:	Fire
Corresp. Planet/Element:	Mars/Fire
Color:	Emerald Green?
	Red/Red
Shape/Quality/Element:	Spherical and Full-to-capacity objects
	Fire

Condition: The only places the Jupiter line can be problematic are in the dining room and possibly the kitchen. It is important to soften this energy in eating locations to avoid feeling so *full* that your waistline expands.

Ideas: Cool the Fire, especially in the kitchen where there may be many accidents. Put up a wine or glass rack, and allow Chi to circulate through it.

Condition: All other areas will benefit by the supply of Jupiter energy.

Ideas: In the wealth area, find a treasure chest and start a collection of coins from all your travels. Fill it so full that some of them fall out, adding an over-abundant decorative element to the table. Have fun as you expand.

Sign:	Capricorn
Symbol:	Goat
Planet:	Saturn
Astrology Element:	Earth
Feng Shui Element:	Fire
Corresp. Planet/Element:	Mars/Fire
Color:	Grey & Black?/Red/Yellow
Shape/Quality/Element:	Compressed or aggressively stable Fire and Earth

Condition: Similar to Pluto, be careful when the Saturn line falls exactly across specific task-oriented furniture. This condition may tend to restrict performance. It may feel as if you have a wide tight elastic band around your chest, making breathing difficult.

Ideas: Without directly sitting on Saturn, it is beneficial to make this planet your friend. If you have the focus, this energy will give you the discipline to complete your tasks. Study in a big (the stability of Earth) leather (Fire generates Earth) chair.

Add Earth/Fire plants[30] in ceramic containers in the Bagua areas where you would like to have additional discipline and perseverance. Plants radiate their own positive Chi and are beneficial in providing fresh air for greater mental clarity. Position them so they do not block Chi or deter pedestrian walkways.

Sign:	Aquarius
Symbol:	Water Bearer
Planet:	Uranus
Astrology Element:	Air
Feng Shui Element:	Wood
Corresp. Planet/Element:	----
Color:	Blue aqua?/Blue, Purple and Black
Shape/Quality/Element:	Odd Shapes/Air

Condition: Be careful when Uranus falls across a task line. The energy, when it is focused while you are sitting directly on the line, may cause instability. This air sign may produce thoughts that are so high-minded or erratic that mentally oriented tasks never get accomplished. There is just too much electricity.

Ideas: Ground your thoughts with Earth energy (destructive cycle). Place a yellow flat bar dot on the wall, just as you did in the Cancer example.

---

[30] This is a hard combination to describe. What I see in my mind's eye is a flower arrangement that is tightly arranged (Constricted Saturn) in a ceramic container full of red heliconia flowers (they look like flames). It is grounded but motivated.

Condition: By enhancing focused Uranian thought, this energy can create unique ideas, that when shared, can change the planet for higher spiritual good.

Ideas: Find a quiet work place in the Uranus room. Be quiet with yourself. Tap into the collective whole and ask about your soul purpose. What do you love doing that can be expanded to help transform consciousness, beginning with yourself? Catch 69! The age of Aquarius is upon us.

Place symbols connected to higher dimensions around the room to help you focus. Do mandalas help you feel connected?

Sign:	Pisces
Symbol:	Fish
Planet:	Neptune
Astrology Element:	Water
Feng Shui Element:	Wood
Corresp. Planet/Element:	Jupiter/Fire
Color:	Purple?/Green/Black
Shape/Quality/Element:	Changing/Water

Condition: Be careful about sitting exactly on the Neptune line. The energies of all the higher octave planets (Uranus, Neptune and Pluto) are spiritually higher-minded and multi-dimensional. When a person cannot differentiate between higher-minded and physical energy, that person has difficulty performing earthly tasks. They are always *out there*.

Neptune specifically tends to distort perception. It is as if you are looking at the world through a glass of water.

Ideas: Stay grounded. The next time you go to a sidewalk art show, look for a playful ceramic fish wearing clothes. Lighten the depths.

As with all the higher octave planets, use deep rich colors to experience the jewels of the soul.

What are your ideas?
Use your creativity to change the energies!

As discussed in Chapter 5, to develop what is best for the entire family, use the color scheme and local space chart for the primary members of the household. The primary individuals, such as the mother and father in the traditional family, set the energy for the entire space. Then, by overlaying the individual charts of each child, you can determine what space will be most beneficial to them.

Because we have all of the components of the zodiac in each of our charts, we experience all of them within us. Through Astrology, we can experience our individuality and connection to everything and everyone else. Like the scales of Libra, we can personify our search for greater balance and harmony.

"Have nothing in your houses that you do not know to be useful, or believe to be beautiful."

William Morris

Conventional Interior Design

Synthesis

How do these various practices relate to each other? As with all forms of geomancy, they share similar natural laws, which have been observed, recognized, and tested through time. When combined with conventional interior design, another dimension is added to your environment that becomes a healthy, supportive second-skin.

The Earth Design process is similar to putting together a puzzle. There are many pieces that purposely fit together to form the whole picture. Conceptually, Earth Design is a three-dimensional experience and each decision requires many considerations.

There are numerous questions about each of the pieces and their relationship to each other. The more experience and greater intuitive awareness you have, the easier it is for the right considerations to arise.

For example:

> You have found the *perfect* piece, and it is on sale. When it is delivered, you realize that the piece is too big and sticks out into the traffic flow area, causing multiple disharmonies and imbalance.

While it is impossible to anticipate all the errors of design, this chapter is about many basic principles that you will need to put together your functional, three-dimensional puzzle.

Form Follows Function

I cannot stress these words of master architect Louis Sullivan enough. The concept is direct. Why design a space that doesn't satisfy your needs? What difference does it make that you spent thousands of dollars on a beautiful space if it doesn't serve you? The first and most important step in any design project is called *Programming*.

What are your needs?

This question may sound too obvious, but all too often I hear, "I wish I had. . .," or "I forgot. . . " The following exercise will help you to remember.

Exercise: *Start a list, and label the various areas you need. Under each area, write down all of the tasks that happen within the individual areas. In your mind's eye, experience the different functions of each space. Then, set priorities, based upon the available space. What areas will need to be multi-purpose?*

Develop a circles within circles[1] schematic, which is known as a "bubble diagram." Decide which room is best for your son, based upon the architectural layout as well

---

[1] This sounds like a sacred mandala, doesn't it?

as his Feng Shui and Astrological evaluation. Then, include everything that happens in his room. Put yourself in your son's shoes, and try to recall everything he does on a daily and weekly basis. Draw circles where he will sleep, dress, study, and play.

Begin to draw a scaled space plan with the actual dimensions of the furnishings needed inside the circles. Is there enough space to accommodate all of those requirements?

It is easy and inexpensive to make changes on paper. Learn to prioritize and compromise.

Once your floor plan is completed, you can begin to consider other pieces of the puzzle, such as life safety.

life Safety

Meeting local building codes for life safety is critical. These codes are designed and regulated by local building departments to ensure that construction conforms with life safety standards.

Most cities require drawings to be approved by registered architects and engineers who understand the codes. With a *sealed architectural* drawing, each expert in the structural, mechanical, electrical, and zoning departments will confirm that the drawings are according to code. Upon their approval, a permit will be issued, and construction may begin. During the construction process, there are scheduled inspections by department officials to verify that the structure is being built according to the approved plans and codes.

Besides possible fines for not conforming to local regulations, there are many things that could go wrong to affect safety. There is also much to know about construction. Please consult a professional to avoid costly and potentially hazardous conditions.

It is important to have good working relationships with your architect and contractors. If you are able to clearly explain your functional needs, their expertise will add pieces to the puzzle. They should ask questions you may not have considered that may enhance the project. Now is the time to insist that all your needs are met, including the use of personally and globally-friendly materials.

As you recall, toxicities, out-gassing, and detrimental electromagnetic conditions can affect your health. You also learned that it is easier to research and commit to using healthy materials while your space is under construction.

At present, there is no correlation between what is acceptable to governmental *life safety* and *health safety* concerns regarding building materials. Most governmental codes do not address Bau-biology and *green*[2] considerations.

There are more discrepancies than can be mentioned between what are health/life safety concerns and the codes. For example, *Class A* fire retardant carpet and fabrics are essential in non-residential applications. However, the synthetic materials used in fabrication and the chemicals used in the fire retardency process, including formaldehyde, give off toxic fumes even under normal conditions.

Fortunately, awareness of these hazards is increasing. Recently, there was a $2.9 million court-awarded judgement against a floor adhesive[3] manufacturer. The case proved the manufacturer's product was the direct cause of an incurrable ailment. The jury found the manufacturer guilty because the contents list did not reveal all the ingredients or potential health hazards of the product.

What can you do to make a change? Do not settle for purchasing unhealthy products. You can make a difference in planetary conservation

---

[2] *Green* refers to the use of non-toxic materials, environmental qualities, and consideration of electromagnetic exposure.

[3] This adhesive is used to install carpet or sheet vinyl.

and personal health. You have the ability to make changes through grass roots efforts when you do a little extra work.

Research the products under consideration. If consumers are going to purchase environmentally safe and healthy products, manufacturers have to make the necessary changes to meet industry demands. They will have to provide us with more choice, availability, and competitive pricing. Additionally, when manufacturers fabricate healthy products in environmentally safe ways, they too work toward global healing.

Educate elected governmental officials. In order for them to stay in office, make them work for changes in the codes so that healthy materials are included. Remember, by healing your individual environments, you heal on all levels, which extends to everything you encounter and beyond.

> "The difference now, with this generation, is that we are
> ready to do it consciously and to accelerate the process."[a]

Catch 69!

This is an uphill climb with anticipated resistance, but the battle can be won. Just like laws requiring the food industry to label all packaged food with nutrition facts, a healthy materials law will provide us with more freedom of choice.

Designers' Need to Educate

There are major differences between *interior design* and *decorating* services. Similar to architects, designers go through an extensive educational process requiring them to understand life safety concerns. To help the consumer understand the difference, states are passing laws requiring designers to take extensive exams for licensure.

When it comes to *interior* design, there is a fine line between architectural and design services. Both licensed interior designers and architects are capable of providing such life safety considerations as space planning, emergency egress routes, lighting specifications, and appropriate non-hazardous and non-toxic building materials.

An architect would not need the services of an interior designer from a legal perspective, and he/she may not *think* one is needed from a design perspective either. However, interior designers have sensitivities that many architects do not. Interior designers have working experience with current trends and product knowledge. Select credible designers and architects that are sensitive to your needs. The process is a marriage that requires understanding by all parties to produce a successful project. Feel comfortable; communication is everything.

Whether or not the size of your project requires a professional, you still need to understand:

Shape, Scale, Proportion & Negative Space

Structures with completeness are in balance and encourage Chi flow. All form is according to rhythm and proportion. Irregular shapes suppress and limit Chi. There are no irregular shapes in nature. Thus, square and rectangular shapes are best for rooms, apartments, offices, buildings and lot configurations as they allow the greatest design flexibility.[4]

Do you remember the sacred mathematic relationships of nature, Platonic Solids, and ancient architecture? With an understanding of Yin-Yang, your intuition should verify that if part of a structure is disproportionate to the building, it is not in balance and remedies should be taken.

There are no missing pieces.

There is a very important Earth Design principle called *negative space*. Negative space is the *void of Yin-Yang*. This void has dimension that fills

---

[4] An irregular-shaped building, floor plan, or furnishing plan is very difficult to design. The irregularity becomes a requirement to solve, almost at the expense of function. Often the solution is to make it fit, as compared to finding the best solution based upon ALL the design criteria.

your home and work environment the same way it adds to the humanness of your being.

Art is the expression of the human experience, and negative space occurs in all art forms. Negative space is what Master Lao Tzu defines as the *emptiness of being*. In music, negative space is the silence between the notes. In painting, negative space is the white or mass of solid on a canvas. In sculpture, it is in the air space that forms the design, and in architecture, negative space is the space between the columns of a Greek temple.

I call negative space *breathing room* because it is the inhalation of breath before we begin to speak. Negative space is essential in Earth Design because it allows the breath of Chi to circulate through space. Negative space allows our eyes to rest between design features and affords us the opportunity to appreciate the details.

There is a major design difference between *filling the hole* with negative space and leaving the space empty. Negative space is purposefully created by the presence of other well-placed features. It is easy to experience negative space in this two-dimensional plan view.[5]

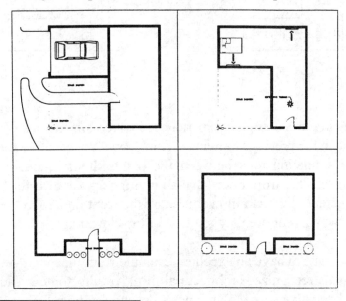

---

[5] Notice where a mirror is placed inside this cleaver-shaped building to bring the task off the detrimental cutting-knife edge of the structure.

Appropriate design features such as plants or light posts are used to define the corners of the negative space without filling the area. Learn to recognize negative space and imbalance in *elevation,* which is also in two-dimension. Note the asymmetrical balance when a rail is added to the elevation in the sketch below. Asymmetrical balance has much greater design interest and can easily be accomplished by using the sacred triangle rule. Can you visualize the triangles in the elevations in this residence and office building?

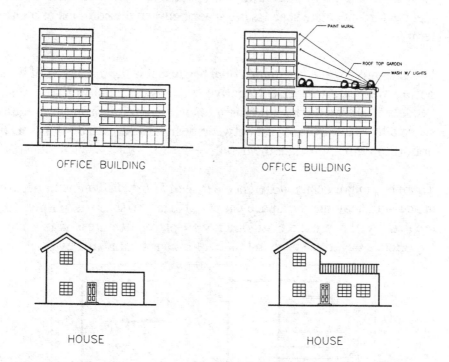

OFFICE BUILDING   OFFICE BUILDING

HOUSE   HOUSE

Everything in Earth Design is experienced in three-dimensions. Visualize the volume in the previous drawings. Think about the negative space and proportional relationships between the plants, house, windows, and walkway. Does the front door have an inviting appearance for Chi and guests to enter? Is there a light source by the front door? Do the plants crowd the window or are they too tall for the elevation?

We are fortunate to have an excellent example from the award-winning, internationally recognized architectural firm, Arquitectonica. They have interpreted negative space in an innovative and sculptural way. Perhaps you will remember seeing the condominium "The Atlantis" [b] (Progressive Architecture Award, 1980) in *Miami Vice* or in the movie *Scarface*. The several-story *sky court* in the center cuts all the way through the building. This functional space was designed for the residents to enjoy the whirlpool while viewing the city below.

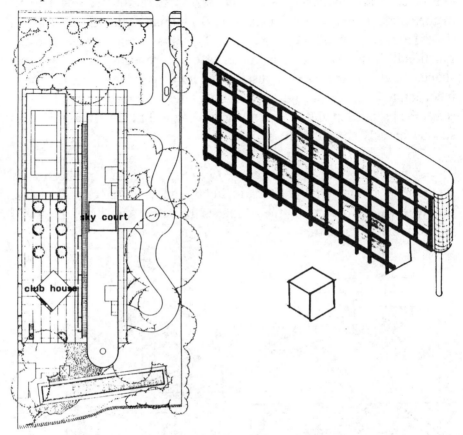

To create harmonious balance, whether or not Arquitectonica consciously used the principles of natural law, the void of the sky court is filled by the club house at ground level that has the same shape, scale, and proportion as the negative space sky court.

Perhaps this example stretches the concept in application; however, the design is creatively functional, and *style* becomes a matter of subjectivity. The design challenges our perceptions and expands the realms of possibilities which allow us to grow.

Ergonomics

You read about spiritual geometry and the *Golden Section* proportion in our brief study of sacred architecture. As a reminder, this natural mathematical law defines the parameters of human scale.[6] Ergonomics is the relationship of human scale to design that is incorporated in the functional design of products. When sacred proportion of archetypal shapes and symbolism is used, *spiritual ergonomics* has been incorporated into the design. Although a Greek temple is very large in scale, the proportion and details are according to Phi, and therefore, it is subconsciously comfortable.

The spiritual ergonomics of *Leo's Man* remind us that proportion is symbolic of humanitarian factors, including universal psyche and spirit. We will feel at home in these spaces because we share the same proportional relationships.

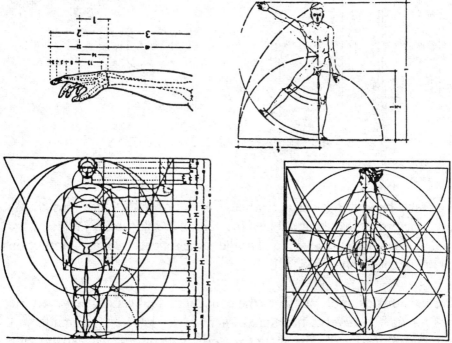

"Man is the measure of all things."

---

[6] The relationship of Phi is indicated by; AB to BC, which is that of the Golden Mean.

Today, everything is designed according to ergonomics: our homes, offices, furniture, equipment, automobiles, and even kitchen utensils. Ergonomics defines the scale and design of items to make them easy to use. The clay vessels the ancients used for storage were possibly some of the first ergonomically-designed items. When the vessels needed to be transportable, they had to be scaled properly so they could be carried when full. Rectangular-shaped bricks were scaled in proportion to the human hands that made them.

Besides the need for Spiritual Ergonomics, conventional ergonomic design considerations are extremely important. They include the height of the kitchen counter, the height of the overheads above the counter, and the height our arms can reach. In the office environment, significant ergonomic attention should be paid to such specialized requirements as seating and computer usage.

Ergonomics is important to consider because it defines the proportion, scale, and functional requirements of a space. What kind of spaces are there? There are intimate spaces, grand spacious areas, and many variables between. Always consider how the space will *feel* in relation to the task. While a high ceiling is elegant in a living room or an entry, a ceiling of the same height in a powder room, no matter how glamorous, will make people feel as if they are in an elevator shaft.

When a desk is designed to maximize function, the scale is according to the human body. The shape will be rectangular, as in a standard-size 30" x 60" or 36" x 72" desk.[7] In an irregular-shaped room, the negative space required for a person to get around a desk for good traffic flow or for

---

[7] Many interior designers use 24" deep work surfaces instead of 30" or 36" for optimum function because our arms can only comfortably reach 24 inches in front of us.

Test it yourself; look at any desk in your office. I guarantee the furthest six inches (on a 30"x 60" desk) or twelve inches (on a 36"x 72" desk) is full of unnecessary clutter.

Because space is expensive, when you save six to twelve inches per each appropriately designed workstation, you often have room for another person who has greater value to the organization than the unnecessary desk space.

guest chairs is either illogical or disproportionately oversized, creating a great deal of expensive wasted space, in addition to being traditionally bad luck.

Finishes should be scaled in proportion to the item or size of the area they cover. Finishes refer to anything that covers a surface, such as paint, wall or floor covering, and fabric. Consider the imbalance of fabric with a big pattern on a small antique vanity stool, 4" x 4" ceramic tile for other than a small bathroom, or a small patterned wall paper on a large wall.

Before making final decisions, visualize the finish in the scale that it will be used. Surely you know someone who painted a room and said, "I didn't know it was going to look like *this* from the chip in the store." Without experience, it is easy to make similar mistakes. Add another easy step to save you any disappointment, redo expense, or additional labor.

When working with finishes, the most reliable test is to experience a large sample in the area it will be used. Only buy a quart of paint (instead of 20 gallons) and apply a large sample in an inconspicuous area. Get a big piece of wallpaper and tape it on the wall, a big piece of carpet or several pieces of tile and lay them on the floor, or a big piece of fabric to drape on the chair.[8] Live with the sample on the area or item and in relation to everything else. To avoid costly mistakes, do not proceed until you are sure. Easy.

The Look

The look refers to the *human expression of design style*. Style is reflected in the historical progression of man. Through human experience, intuition, creativity, efforts, and ingenuity, man has designed functional and aesthetic tools to accommodate ergonomics.

Style refers to the influence of politics and philosophy on the arts. Throughout civilization, style has been a distinctive expression influenced by mysticism and mythology. This distinction can be seen by the symbols on Egyptian furniture dating as far back as 1400 BC or on

---

[8] Most suppliers make large loaner samples available for approval.

the legs of early 19th century French/American Empire furniture. Throughout the ages, the look has become a symbol of wealth (ornateness of Rococo and Baroque), spiritual and utilitarian simplicity (Shaker), and every expressive fashion trend between.

Today's look incorporates a multitude of buzz words such as Country French, Art Deco, Post Modern, and so forth. Whatever style is represented by these words is not a true representation of the *period pieces* designed by the master artisans. Because of this condition, it is impossible to suggest that Earth Design represents any particular style. Earth Design is a physical manifestation of the progressing human experience.

> "These arts were merely the result of a natural desire on the part of the people with aesthetic joys or a deeper significance or were the result of religious spiritual impulses." [c]

Earth Design is representative of personal expression.

Individual pieces of furniture, art, and accessories blended in a harmonious manner express the energy of personal style. By surrounding yourself in your own *style*, your well-being, individuality, and greatness of purpose is enhanced.

If pressed for a definition, the style of Earth Design would have to be called *Eclectic,* which is a harmonious combination of many styles. There is no comparison between hodgepodge and eclectic. Hodgepodge is reminiscent of a college dormitory. Do you remember those designer concrete block and wood plank shelving systems?

Eclectic is the conscious selection of pieces that you love. By placing those pieces together in a skillful way, personal style is created. Eclectic design may even be symbolic of Earth Design as the intertwined balance of natural law through which you express yourself.

To develop a look of your own, begin by being aware of your design taste. Start a file of pictures cut out from design magazines. Though furniture showrooms feature mainstream products and creativity, notice how the room displays are put together. As an exercise, think about what you could do to add your creativity. As you gain experience, your sensitivity and ability to put different styles together will increase.

Never assume that one piece will not work with another. Do you love it? Where can you put it? Can you make it work? When it is considered in good taste, an *avant garde* piece may become a great *Where did you find it?* accent.

If you have put thought and intuition into the design, placed furniture properly, developed a coordinated color scheme, included good form, a nice blend of textures, and proper proportion and scale, your very own style will be perfect. **You will be proud of your efforts!**

Color

Color is a science with profound depth and complexity that has been the subject of many books. The use of color in Earth Design is similar to that of style. Where style may be a combination of many ideas, there should be compatibility between color relationships. Through a color-coordinated scheme, you pull together different styles and textures.

A color scheme should be carried throughout your home or office. When a cohesive color concept runs throughout a space, it becomes a unified entity. Each room, whether or not it is physically touching another, needs to be part of the whole.[9]

Color scheme is color harmony.

---

[9] An exception to this concept would be the rooms for children. While children are part of the family, their rooms should assert their individuality based upon their Earth Design profile.

A working home office is also considered as a separate entity and could reflect the ambiance of the business.

By changing the quality of the colors, they can be used throughout as a unifying ribbon. Let's use the color combination of red, aqua, and purple in an elegant way throughout a house:

The Foyer: An off-white marble floor with a gilded (or gold patina paint) metal-framed console with an aqua green/black marble top

Living room: Sophisticated natural-colored, high-textured raw silk (or fine cotton) in jewel-tone purple and aqua with a touch of red; high-textured solid accents in purple, aqua, and red

Family room: Whimsy, bold, playful colors and patterns on cotton canvas

Master bedroom: Lilac, dusty rose, and light aqua in subtle patterns with feminine white eyelet and lace.

This *pretend* client is not available for comment on these *unselected* fabrics. Remember, a color scheme is determined from the visual experience of all fabrics, not through the interpretation of something unseen. The important issue is not if this color scheme is appropriate for you, but for you to understand how the qualities and flexibility of color can be used as a unifying thread.

When you are developing a color scheme including horoscope or Bagua remedies, it is important to use good color sense. Some people instinctively have it. For those of you that do not, begin to develop it by exposing yourself to good color combinations.

Please be sensitive! Just because your shirt and pants are blue, it does not mean the *blues* work together. They may even clash. What do you think clashing colors will do for your emotional and spiritual well-being?

Test your instincts regarding color combinations by looking around at fabrics. Notice how color is combined. If your combination is good, most likely you will see something similar through a fabric designer's interpretation.

Try to remove yourself from marketing trends. Designing a color palette for your home has greater longevity that buying an Easter dress, so use careful consideration and judgement.

> When I develop a color scheme for a client, I don't consider the *in* colors. They will be *out* shortly in order for the *new* colors to come *in.* What are your colors and in what combination will they be harmonious?

Pay attention to the background color (perhaps it is the major color in your astrological chart), along with the accent colors that make up the pattern or texture. Find a suitable fabric with all of your colors.[10] Perhaps that favorite can be the *starter fabric* from which all the other finishes and furnishings will be coordinated.

> *When I am developing a color scheme for a client, I always get an approval on a starter fabric. "Do you like the tones, the style and scale of the pattern, and the texture?" If the answer is "No," I find other selections with the same colors. I hold on to all of them because they may be more appropriate as coordinates or for another room. By using this process, your solids, coordinating patterns, finishes, and furnishings will fall into place.*

Remember to integrate all Earth Design principles to complete the puzzle.

If you are helping someone determine their color scheme, use your intuitive abilities combined with theirs. Have them go through the astrological exercise in Chapter 6. By sensitively working together and setting the intent, the appropriate color scheme will develop.

---

[10] When selecting fabric, confirm that it can be used for what you have intended. Fabric that is suitable for a dress is not designed for sofa upholstery. Drapery fabric may or may not be suitable for upholstery. Don't forget to consider durability appropriate to usage.

In the event that you are rebelling against the *Astrology of Color* and would like to ignore it, go ahead. Find a starter fabric that you love. Whatever you select, the colors are somehow a part of who you are. One day, should you decide to check out the astrological relationship, please let me know what you discover.

There is one other consideration about color that you should know. Both warm and cool colors need to be incorporated in your design. Warm colors, such as reds, oranges, browns, and yellows, radiate heat from the earth or the sun. Cool colors, like blues, greens, and grays, have the feeling of absorption, like being swallowed by the ocean. Purple falls in between because it is a combination of both warm/red and cool/blue.

Here's an easy exercise:

> *If only warm colors are used, a space will feel _____; if only cool colors are used, the space will feel _____.*

Although you may have a specific reason for a space to feel either warm or cold, always add a proportional percentage of the other color group for psychological balance.[11] It will probably be the perfect accent needed to make a color scheme that much better.

Lighting

Lighting in Earth Design complies with natural law. Through observation, day changes to dusk and transforms into night. You will notice the variables of light as it changes *depth, color, perception, texture,* and *form.* In an environment, light can be used as a vehicle of design and perception.

Lighting is a science unto itself. My intent is to provide you with an understanding of its complexity to add to your Earth Design education.

---

[11] This is analogous to the white/black dot in the Yin/Yang.

As a project enters this phase, you will be knowledgeable enough to know when additional research[12] or consideration may be required.

Light is the most important consideration of any art form. Second to life safety, lighting influences everything else more than any other principle. Light is radiant energy that excites the retina in the eye, allowing us to see. Light provides shadow for depth perception, form, and color. Color is reflected light that is either absorbed or refracted by various objects. This characteristic will be a factor in design decisions.

Use the percentage of light reflected from *the walls & ceilings chart* [d] to give you ideas.

Percent of light reflected from typical walls & ceilings

Class	Surface	Color	Percentage of light reflected
Light	Paint	White	81
	Paint	Ivory	79
	Paint	Cream	74
	Stone	Cream	69
Medium	Paint	Buff	63
	Paint	Light green	63
	Paint	Light gray	58
	Stone	Gray	56
Dark	Paint	Tan	48
	Paint	Dark gray	26
	Paint	Olive green	17
	Paint	Light oak	32
	Paint	Dark oak	13
	Paint	Mahogany	8
	Cement	Natural	25
	Brick	Red	13

---

[12] There are many sources available to get more information about light levels, foot candles, lumens, wattage, and various bulb types.

From the chart, you can see why it is possible that a higher wattage bulb may be necessary for a room painted a deep color. Consider the task to the relationship of light and glare. Does the fixture make allowances for the type and wattage that will give off enough light for the task? Will the fixture and bulb produce appropriate light for reading, cooking, or toasting champagne?

Because most of your spaces are multi-tasked, lighting allows flexibility to alter the ambient mood. This flexibility is easily accomplished by having several different light sources. Good lighting design incorporates fixtures that have various light distribution qualities.

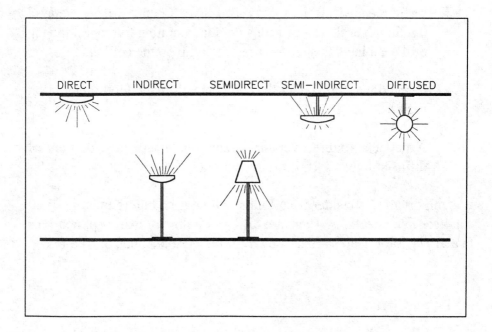

In the Family room:

A *torchere* is not only a creative design element, but the light floods the ceiling and provides indirect illumination.

A table lamp directs light for reading as it features an accessory on the table.

Directly focused light can accent a piece of art on the wall and provide design interest.

Wall sconces, on either side of a fireplace or painting, are conventional accents that provide decorative indirect light.

By putting the fixture on dimmers and turning some on/off you can create different moods. Keep in mind that dimmers turn the light yellow as they dim. Experiment.

In the Kitchen:

To illuminate the entire space, a direct luminous ceiling is recommended; it is the typical way kitchens have general lighting. It is also nice to consider incorporating fixtures at the top of the cabinets to shoot indirect light up on the ceiling.

Direct down-light under the cabinets will make food preparation easier.

A pendent fixture over the kitchen table will provide general diffused light for comfortable eating.

It is important to consider what bulbs will be used before making final color scheme selections. There are different bulbs for many applications that affect color. Bulbs are designed for the various kinds of fixtures.

Use the following chart[e] to help you:

Color Rendition

Color		Interior			Exterior		Low Voltage
							Interior/Exterior
	Cool White Incandescent	**Warm White Florescent**	**Deluxe White Florescent**	**Mercury Vapor**	**High Pressure Sodium**	**Metal Halide**	**Halogen***
red	grayish red	red	grayish red	red	rust red orange	dull red	red
orange	orange	grayish orange	slight yellow orange	yellow orange	dark yellow	orange	orange
yellow	yellow	light greenish yellow	yellow	light yellow	yellow	yellow	yellow
green	green	green	green	grayish green	blue green	green	green
blue	blue	blue	blue violet	dark blue	dark blue violet	blue	blue
violet	violet	violet	violet	light blue violet	brownish violet	violet	violet
brown	brown	brown	grey brown	brown	golden yellow brown	brown	brown
(light) skin	ruddy	pale	natural yellowish	pale tan	suntan look	pale	natural
(dark) skin	natural	grayish brown	brown	grayish brown	brown	pale	natural

A good rule before your final color selection is to look at the combination of finishes: paint, textiles, wood finishes, and so forth, in the same light that you will be using. If you are using fluorescent light with warm white bulbs, make the final selection under those conditions. If you don't, the color scheme may look different from what you originally intended.

In the event the same type of lighting is not readily available, consider this trick. Go into the natural sunlight with your finishes. When all of the colors work together in natural light, all of the colors will work together in whatever lighting is chosen. The overall palette may look different, but all the colors will coordinate with each other.

Designers favor halogen lamps because they render color in its truest value, shade, and hue (as you can see in the graph), because their light quality is the most similar to natural light. Often halogen lamps are used in low-voltage fixtures. Beyond color purity, low-voltage fixtures have multiple advantages. Because the bulbs are so small, there are many great-looking fixtures. Low voltage lighting is more energy efficient, the lamps last longer, and the light quality does not fade with age.

Low voltage fixtures require transformers, which are often designed in the base of the fixture. The transformer steps down the current between the 120-volt electrical wall outlet and the 12 low-volt fixture. Transformers give off high concentrations of electromagnetic energy (see Chapter 3). Consider the rules: sources of electromagnetic energy should be a minimum of an arm's length away to reduce long-term exposure. There is nothing wrong with a transformer in a fixture base sandwiched between a sofa and love seat in an "L" configuration. Make sure the rebars in the foundation or metal studs in the wall are not channeling the radiation all over the house.

Use intuition to help design with light. Consider what happens when you are driving at night. Aren't your eyes automatically attracted to the lights of oncoming traffic? Place the brightest illumination on a featured item. Is there a special sculpture or piece of art that sets the tone for the entire room?

In lighting design, usually the fixture is an integral part of the design. Sometimes designs may incorporate light with concealed fixtures. These fixtures are designed for utility only and are typically less expensive. It is the light that is important. Using lighting in this way creates interest and design sophistication.

Consider how light will affect surfaces. What kind of patterns will it make? A series of recessed eyeball high hats in a ceiling will create *light scallops* on a wall. Do you want the light to be *pooled*, have purposeful *hot spots*, or gently wash an area? Light can be used in many artistic ways. Be creative.

There are even some fixtures designed to make light into art. While the fixture itself may or may not be designed as a feature, light radiates out creating beautiful patterns on the wall or ceiling.[13] When you go to a

---

[13]   I have used low profile fixtures with a fine beam spread that puts a corporate logo of light on the floor in an entry vestibule. It is impressive.

lighting showroom, ask the sales person to show you some of these fixtures. Make sure to turn off the surrounding fixtures so you can appreciate the full effect.

When considering lighting, remember scale and proportion. Light sources need to be at the height appropriate to the task. Pay attention to this rule so you won't be affected by glare. Usually, if you select the fixture properly and use the recommended bulbs, you will avoid glare.

The good news is that lighting is an exciting asset to any design. The bad news is it is usually more expensive than you have budgeted. Plan accordingly.

Budget/Design Process/Longevity

The first part of the Earth Design process is to get started. Money isn't required to practice Earth Design. What does it cost to start planning, doodle on your floor plan, or cut pictures out of magazines? There are many things that can be done with what you have around the house.

> Move the furniture around to enhance Chi flow and harmonize the energetics of the elements.

> What accessories do you have that can be placed more beneficially?

> Is there any leftover paint in the garage that can be used in an auspicious way?

> Can you put the vase in a favorable Gua?

> Are there any flowering plants in your garden to put in the vase?

> Do you have any fabric that can be draped in a creative way?

> Do the kids have play money? Sprinkle coins in the wealth area of your yard.

Make a hanging mobile out of sea shells collected at the beach.

Clean the glass/crystal on the lighting fixtures.

Repair or replace anything broken.

If you have chosen to spend just a few hundred dollars, there are still many things that can make a difference. Paint is the least expensive and most wonderful design medium. It is forgiving too; if you make a mistake, simply repaint. Play with the energetics of color. After considering the labor costs, even with labors of love, buy the best paint that you can afford. The better the paint, the longer it will look good, and the longer it will last.

Buy things that are going to make the biggest energetic impact and use them properly. How much is a wind chime, faceted crystal ball, or mirror? Get the children some fish, and make their care a family project. Watch for sales at housewares and department stores. They have colored pillows, brass accents (Metal), glassware accessories (Water), and pottery (Earth).

Think about how much fun you can have going to garage sales or flea markets looking for old mirrors or interesting objects to use in your creative efforts.

Recently I bought a round iron bird cage for a dollar. When I filled it with live ivy, it became a nice Metal accent with live Chi.

Set a budget if you plan to make a larger financial investment. For most of us, not setting a budget means a project will never be completed because we have not prioritized.

Presuppose everything will cost more than you have and more than it should. It usually does. Always do your homework and confirm that the products under consideration are priced according to industry standards and quality.

Decide how much money you want to spend now and in the future. You may find it helpful to back into this decision after the budget is completed. Plan the budget in the same way that a designer will help a client prioritize the project, based upon affordability and financial priority. Separate the project into monetary phases. Phases are helpful for several reasons:

Most of us do not have enough money to do the whole project simultaneously.

Allocated monies can be concentrated into distinct areas and completed over time.

I recommend that you finish one area before starting a new one. This will allow you to visualize the *whole* by using one area as a sample. If you did a little in all the areas, the effects would be spread too thin. It would appear that nothing was happening.

I suggest completing a *public space* first, such as the living, dining, or family room. That way, the physical, emotional, and spiritual effects of Earth Design can be shared by all occupants and guests. These are probably the rooms that require the largest budget because of their size and function.

Begin to prioritize your budget, based upon the look and quality you want. The best way to set monetary priorities is to plan the job in advance. Budgetary planning is the business part of the process.

The first step is to prepare a line item analysis. To avoid cost over-run surprises, everything should be broken down by quantity. Consider each item, including square yards of carpeting, single/double rolls of wallcovering, and yards of fabric for each piece of furniture. Add shipping and freight, delivery and set up, such mechanics' fees as electricians, painters, or wallpaper hangers, and applicable sales tax. Request written quotations from workmen and suppliers. These confirmations will verify pricing when the purchase or service order is placed.

Again, review your decisions before placing any orders.

Exercise: *Close your eyes. In your mind's eye, walk into the area you have designed and visualize everything in three-dimension. Experience the volume and relationships between the floor, walls, and ceiling. Look at the way the furniture is laid out. Is there enough room to safely walk? Are peoples' knees going to bump when they are seated? How do the colors, fabrics, textures, and patterns look together?*

How does the light dance in the space, and how is it affecting everything else? Visualize it. See every detail. How does it look? ***How is the Chi? How does your home Feel?***

How do you feel about your accomplishment? When you are satisfied, make it happen.

When you are placing orders, have the suppliers include: *all* possible charges, the amount of your deposit (typically 50%), warranties, and estimated delivery dates.[14] This written order will protect both you and the vendor.

By putting the delivery date on the order, it will not only make the vendor accountable, but it will help you organize progressive deliveries and installations. When everything starts to come in, you'll probably be too excited to remember to request maintenance and cleaning instructions, so get them now. If you file them with the warranties, they will be readily available.

Once lead times are established, calendar when everything is expected. Compile a delivery schedule based upon the logical progression of installations. Wallcovering and paint should be completed before carpet is laid, ceramic tile is installed before wallcovering, and flooring is obviously installed before furnishings.

---

[14] Industry standards could be anywhere from 8-12 weeks and possibly longer.

What happens when the wallcovering is back-ordered and it disrupts the installation schedule? Select another that is readily available or wait. It needs to be hung before laying the carpet.

It is possible that you cannot find what you had in mind for a certain piece or area. Go ahead and order everything anyway. If you put the allocated money aside, the cash will be available when it is found. Even if the rest of the items have been installed and the piece is missing, do not worry. You have set the energy. Do not settle. This is a major financial undertaking that needs to make you happy and be supportive for a long time. Wait, and the right piece will show up.

For such major pieces as dining tables and chairs, sofas, consoles, buffets, and desks, buy good quality with a classic design. Consider that the quality should last a lifetime. Check the construction. Is the piece finished properly, easily maintained, and how will it hold up to sea air if you live by the ocean?

When you purchase major items with a classic design style, your design may be changed without having to repurchase the major pieces. It is not expensive or difficult to repaint the walls a new color, change accessories and accents, or reupholster the soft items.

> *I am reminded of a friend and a coffee table. The table was not inexpensive. It was granite with an unfinished edge, nice. On the top, a geometric with bright, high-contrasting colors was painted. It was finished with polyurethane that looked like a thick sheet of plastic. (This technique may be appropriate in a seafood restaurant where they have sand, treasure maps, and doubloons buried in the plastic.)*
>
> *"What a way to ruin a beautiful granite slab. What are you going to do with it when the trend is over and you realize you have wasted your money?"*

Earth Design should be an enjoyable, fun process, and always in motion, just like the natural laws. As you grow, your energetics will expand, and more than likely your tastes will change.

Gimmicks can be fun and whimsical, but make sure they are in good taste. Make sure furnishings and accessories have staying power when a lot of money is at issue. If you like the look of brightly colored geometrics, use them as an accent that allows you future choice should the piece no longer serve you. Can it easily be moved to another area?

Perhaps, buy an inexpensive poster that you don't mind giving away with the understanding that the dollars spent paid for its enjoyment. On the other side of the coin, do your homework, and consider purchasing signed art that has collectable and/or resale value.

As with any *life project* budget, always remember that the universe will provide for you. It is your birthright to have all that you desire. The process of *being full* can only come from within. Abundance comes from your internal reality of knowing this truth and taking action on intuition.

The first natural law and true test for creating good Earth Design is knowing that all is possible. Dr. Deepak Chopra shares this law with such wonderful clarity,

> "When we are grounded in the nature of reality and we
> also know that this same reality is our own nature, then
> we realize that we can create anything, because all of
> material creation has the same origin."[f]

Set the intent!
We have come full circle . . .
and the seasons they go round and round . . .

Part Three

THE TOP FLOOR
Personal Cultivation

*We are all enlightened,
we just need to remember how.*

The Divine Plan

Like the cycles of nature, we have come full circle. From spring's new growth, we have experienced the journey of energetic awareness. By walking the path of the divine plan, we can create a personal life circle of balance and growth. Our own lives are the progression of natural cycles within cycles formed by our own symbolic geometric and archetypal mandala.

We are part of the earth's sacred tradition.

You have seen the natural laws affect us through the how and why of Earth Design. By experimenting with the methods, you have intuitively selected that which personally works best for you to create harmony in your environment and to make a difference in your life.

Earth Design is merely one method to help you develop balance between the physical, emotional, and spiritual life experience. It is not a *quick fix* nor a complete formula for success.

You also should continue to develop your *Personal Chi, trust and follow your intuition, and actively pursue your dreams.*

The Greatest Dimension of Earth Design is the Evolution of your Divine Plan.

For your homes and offices to become sacred places of maximum potential, your spiritual process needs to create the momentum of Catch 69! Then, you can transform ordinary spaces into places of spirit that fully support you.

Spatial Memory

Because of your Earth Design actions, you will feel the positive effects at all times on different vibrational levels. Knowing that everything is energy, when you put your mind, body, and spiritual intention into something, it remains there. It is the same as sharing love with someone; even if the love is lost, the memory of that love is still within you.

Your energy has been put into your environment, and it loves you. The memory of the process will be maintained in the energy of your environment.[1] Even without conscious thought, the *memory* held in the space will continue to support you.

The Evolutionary Energetic

Astrologically speaking, we know that *now* is a time of spiritual awakening. We are entering the *Age of Aquarius*. Whether or not planetary energetics are of interest to you, we are entering a *New Age*. *This surge of higher consciousness is the evolution of the Divine Plan.* Through personal development, we subconsciously combine our energies, spinning together toward the *Neo-Renaissance* of global spiritual awakening. We become seeds in the cycle of our evolving planet. From

---

[1]   Whenever you occupy a new *home,* even if it is a hotel room for the night, it is important to cleanse the space. This is done through the mental process of using your mind's eye to release the energetic memory of the previous occupants.

amebas, to crawlers, to four-leggeds, to two-leggeds, and to what next? It is our evolution. Have you seen the movie *Cocoon?* Are we becoming creatures of light?

While it is interesting to consider our future, we live in the present. Part of this evolution is for us to take time to celebrate the joy of living.

> *I was hiking in Bryce Canyon in the middle of winter. The sky was a clear, bright blue, but the snow was up to my knees. With the elevation changes and having to lift my legs up out of the snow just to take the next step, I was working hard! All my effort was on the work, and I forgot the wonder of where I was.*
>
> *In my thoughts, I had discovered the ultimate step class, and I began to laugh. Hard! I laughed at myself, my joy, and the beauty around me. How could I get so caught up in the work that I forgot?*

Happiness comes from the awareness of such joys of life as the kindness of a gesture, the fragrance of a flower, or the sensation of a breeze. **The personal part of evolution is to celebrate the joy of life.** Sometimes we are so task-driven that we forget. When this happens, we merely need to forgive ourselves and gently bring our awareness back.

We get so caught up in our lives that we are not as nice to each other as we could be. By forgiving and being kinder to ourselves, we develop greater sensitivity to others and become more congenial. By sharing our spirit, we become balanced in our personal cycle and take our place in the larger cycle of planetary evolution.

Symbolic Lessons from Earth Design cures:

> When light passes through a crystal prism, it splits into multiple facets, and a rainbow of color is produced. When spiritual light passes through us, we share our many colors with others. Light passes through a prism in both directions. When others share their

spiritual light with us, it mixes with ours, adding additional strength (and love) to our own.

When light is reflected off a mirror, the light bounces back. What happens when you teach something to others? You get greater confirmation of what you are teaching through their excitement of learning. When we are sharing ourselves, our light gets reflected right back.

These are the tools of energetic evolution. Spiritual energy is nature's glue and the energetic that creates the cycles. The energy that passes through us is the natural law of the Divine plan!

Tools of Energetic Development

As products of nature, we need to tune into the energies of the earth to perpetuate spiritual energetic experiences. There are tools that have proven useful to have better control over energy fields or personal Chi. For example, mind control techniques such as meditation have been shown to increase sensitivity.

We are attached to this physical world, and many of us find it difficult to stay focused in our heads long enough to get much value out of meditation. Perhaps our minds are not disciplined enough to put the *to-do* list aside for a few minutes.

Personally, I have difficulty meditating. However, I can easily keep my mind focused when I am grounded by a physical task. Use your body as part of the spiritual experience; it is of the earth. Many of the personal stories I have shared with you have come from my *spiritual experiences* while taking long hikes in the woods. You may want to try incorporating traditional *body work* such as Thai Chi, Yoga, or martial arts to enhance your mind, body, and spirit.

Learn to tend a garden. Spend time in the dirt. All the lessons are there. Entire life cycles can be experienced. Feel the relationship of the garden to the elements. Learn how nature's wheel is in perfect balance as you become a part of every rock, plant, and weed in your garden. You will even get familiar with the animals and recognize them as old friends.

You can keep a journal. Meditations in your head are focused and grounded by the physical experience of writing the words down. Create your own mythology.

Surround yourself with like-minded people. Share your personal experiences, the books you have read, and what you have learned from inspirational workshops.

Create your own ceremonies for focusing energy. Spend some time staring at a flickering candle to focus yourself. Create *affirmations*[2] and say them upon waking and before going to sleep.

> *"My Earth Design project is wonderful; it will support me as part of my spiritual evolution. I am continuing to experience the lessons of the natural laws as I celebrate the joys of being alive."*

When traveling, learn how to be a *pilgrim* and not just a tourist. What makes a place special is the energy. Do not take it and create a depletion. As a pilgrim, be grateful for the experience and thank the space, thereby leaving a bit of yourself there. Remember, part of the reason why places are sacred is because they hold the memory of all the people who have ever visited them.

Be flexible; allow yourself to get caught up in the experience. The Divine Plan requires that you sometimes need *to let go* to see where spirit and destiny will take you.

> *While traveling in Santa Fe, my husband and I met a very nice woman. When I told her about my work she said, "I do geo-shamantic work too." (Interesting concept: Was I an earth-medicine woman?)*

---

[2]   An affirmation is a positive declaration.

She asked, "Did you check out the EarthShips in Taos? There is an architect building self-sufficient homes out of recycled materials."

Why was I coincidentally finding myself in this conversation? Weeks before, a client and I had talked about designing her home from the ground up,[3] using all Earth Design concepts. Her desire is to build an eight-thousand square-foot home, including sacred geometry, Feng Shui, Astrology, non-toxic materials, as well as energy-conservation and energy-generating systems.

From Santa Fe, we were leaving for Boulder the following day, and Taos was right on the path. Another coincidence? Trusting in the special connection made with this new friend, Joel and I decided to stop.

Upon reaching Taos, we called the management office of Solar Survival Architecture, "Michael Reynolds will be out in the field all day; you are welcome to schedule an appointment for next week."

Knowing that was impossible, we decided to check out the EarthShips. The intent was set; we were going to meet Mr. Reynolds. We arrived at a site under construction, and it blew my mind!

These homes of structural integrity were made from discarded tires and soda cans overlaid with packed earth. Down the road, people were living in them.

Michael Reynolds has designed systems that harvest electricity from the sun and water from precipitation. Part of the design includes a greenhouse area to grow vegetables and to purify the air within the living space.

---

[3] I think this project is really going to happen, so watch for our future book:
Earth Design: Creating a Home from the Ground Up.

Of course, we met him. However, the best part of the day was experiencing the passion he had set in motion. He was teaching people how to build their own EarthShips. All the men and women who were working in harmony with the earth were full of love and the spirit of sharing their joy.

Catch 69!

Reflected Light, Evolution in Taos.
Right there at Home!

Had I not been aware enough to recognize an opportunity so magically presented, I would never have been exposed to what I needed so much to learn.

What a powerful day! I was so in love!

Michael gave to them, they gave to me, and now I can give to you.

This is Energetic Evolution.
This is the Divine Plan.

Greater Wealth, Health, and Happiness

I have so much respect for Michael because he is abundantly rich. While designing EarthShips and teaching others to build them is his business, I am not talking about financial riches.

Michael has not compromised his dream. He is living his destiny. He is an architect, doing what he loves, and sharing it with others.

It is no *coincidence*!
What else is there? This man is alive!

It doesn't matter what you do for a living, what matters is *To Live*!

**Abundance comes from being alive.
It is our birthright to be and to have all that we desire.**

It is a law of nature to blossom into a plentiful tree that shares its fruit.

The universe is magnificently abundant.

**When we follow our Divine Plan,
the Universe will be of service and reward us.**

How wonderful it is to appreciate the masterful design of the Divine Plan. We are fortunate to share what the ancients learned by observation, study, and application. How resourceful we are to recognize and make use of the riches that harmoniously exist for us.

It trust that my sharing will be a seed in our evolution. I set the intent that during our earth walk, we can grow beyond our teachers and continue to add new dimensions to our lives. We have the capacity.

Allow me to affirm, *Let us be kinder to ourselves and others to create a better world as we nurture and have greater respect for our home: Planet Earth.*

And the cycle continues...

About the Author

 Jami Lin is a graduate of the University of Florida School of Architecture. She has been creating Corporate, Financial, Healthcare, Hospitality, and Residential Interiors since 1979.

Jami and her staff of licensed designers focus on maximizing business potential and creating specialized living environments.

Jami Lin's firm, Earth Design, incorporates space planning, sacred architectural form, non-toxic and environmental concerns, life and health safety, barrier-free requirements, computer considerations, personal and environmental energetics, lighting, texture, and color, all within the functional realm of a client's specific needs.

By combining conventional interior design experience and expertise with metaphysics, Jami's clients are taken on a spiritual journey of substance and form as their 21st century lifestyle environments are personalized.

A dynamic speaker, who has been featured in numerous national publications, **Jami Lin is available for private consultations, seminars and workshops.**

Jami and her husband Joel Levy are both Bau-biologists, and are currently living in South Florida.

Slides please: We welcome slides of interior and exterior Earth Design conditions (secret arrows, areas with restricted Chi, bad door configurations, etc.) and your solutions. For any slides we use in our lectures, we will send you a traditional Feng Shui cure along with mirrors.

Thank you!

1. Natural Law

a.   Joni Mitchell, "The Circle Game, Ladies of the Canyon," 1970.

b.   James A. Swan, *The Power of Place & Human Environments: An Anthology*, Theosophical Publishing House, 1991 p. 243.

c.   Tom Porter and Bob Greenstreet, *Graphic arts-Techniques*, Charles Scribner's Sons, 1980, p. 62.

2. Historical Geomancy

a.   Joseph Campbell, *The Mythic Image*, Princeton University Press, 1974 p.99.

b.   Swan, op. cit., "Geomancy," Richard Feather Anderson, p. 192.

c.   John Matthews, *The World Atlas of Divination,* "Consulting the Oracles: The Classic System of Greece and Rome," Robert Temple, Bullfinch Press, 1992, p.70.

d.   Swan, op. cit, "Circle the Earth," Anna Halprin, p. 316.

e.   A. T. Mann, *Sacred Architecture*, Element Books, 1993, p. 15.

f.   Swan, op. cit., "Ancient Theaters as Sacred Space," Rachel Fletcher, p. 90.

g.   Mann, op. cit., p. 21.

h.   Jose and Mirium Arguelles, *Mandala*, Shambala Publications, 1972, p. 12.

i.   Mann, op. cit., p. 25.

j.   Mann, ibid., p. 34.

k.   Nicholas R. Mann, *Sedona: Sacred Earth,* Zivah Publishers, 1989, p. 45.

l.   Ernest Lehner, *Symbols, Signs & Signets*, Dover Publications, 1950, p. 77.

m.   Swan, op. cit., "Circle the Earth," Anna Halprin, p. 316.

n.   Mann, op. cit., p. 105.

o.   Mann, ibid., p. 143.

p.   Mann, ibid., p. 184.

2. Historical Geomancy (cont.)

q.   E. T. Casey, *Frank Lloyd Wright: In the Realm of Ideas,* Frank Lloyd Wright Foundation, Carbondale, Southern Illinois University Press, "Organic Architecture the Principles of Frank Lloyd Wright," Aaron G. Green, FAIA p. 134 .

r.   Casey, ibid., "In Structure in Organic Architecture," p. 156.

s.   Frank Lloyd Wright, *An Organic Architecture,* The Frank Lloyd Wright Foundation, MIT Press, 1970, c. 1939.

3. Natural Science

a.   James Redfield, *The Celestine Prophesy*, Warner Books Printing, 1994, p.149.

b.   Mann, op. cit., pp. 90-91.

c.   Mann, ibid., p. 88.

d.   Swan, op. cit., "The Ley Hunters," Richard Leviton, p. 246.

e.   Swan, ibid., pp. 249-249.

f.   Swan, ibid., "The Rings of Gaia," William S. Becker and Bethe Hagens, p. 259.

g.   Swan, ibid., p 273.

h.   Alden Hatch, *Buckminster Fuller at Home in the Universe*, Crown Publishers, 1974, p. 186.

i.   Hatch, ibid., p. 210.

j.   Swan, op. cit., "Working with the Earth's Electromagnetic Fields," Elizabeth Rauscher, p. 300.

k.   Swan, ibid., p. 288.

l.   R. B. Fuller, *No More Second-Hand God*, Carbondale, Southern Illinois University Press, 1963, p. 82.

m.   Katherine Metz, "The Art of Placement."

n.   Swan, op. cit., p.316.

4. Intuition

a.   Hatch, op. cit., p. 2.

b.   Redfield, op. cit., p. 223.

c.   Hatch, op.cit., p. 151.

d.   Barbara Marciniak, *Bringers of the Dawn, Teachings from the Pleiadians*, Bear & Company, 1993, p. 77.

5. Feng Shui

a.   Derek Walters, *The Feng Shui Handbook*, Aquarian Press, 1991, pp.102-103.

b.   Hua-Ching Ni, *I CHING: The Book of Changes and the Unchanging Truth*, Shrine of the Eternal Breath of Tao, 1983, p.106.

c.   Hua-Ching Ni, ibid., p. 79 and p. 98.

d.   Swan, op. cit., "Feng Shui as Terrestrial Astrology in Traditional China and Korea," David J. Nemeth, p. 225.

e.   Alexander Ruperti, *Cycles of Becoming: The Planetary Pattern of Growth*, CRCS Publications, 1989, p. 171.

6. Astrology

Steve cozzi, *Planets in Locality*, Llewellyn Publications, 1988

a.   Sarah Rossbach, *Interior Design with Feng Shui*, Penguin Group, 1991, p. 27.

7. Conventional Interior Design

a.   Redfield, op. cit., p. 149.

b.   Beth Dunlop, *Arquitectonica*, American Institute of Architects Press, 1991, p. 36. (modified by author for clarification)

c.   Sherrill Whiton, *Interior Design and Decoration,* J. B. Lippincott Company, 1957, p.279.

d.   S. C. Reznikoff, *Interior Graphic and Design Standards*, Whitney Library of Design, p. 309.

e.   Reznikoff, ibid., p. 307, *added by author.

f.   Deepak Chopra, *Creating Affluence: Wealth Consciousness in the Field of Possibilities*, New World Library, 1993, p.17.

Crystal Prisms

Gift Boxed with hanging ribbon
(Think about the size required proportionate to the Cure!)

Octagonal

	Size		Each	Total
_____quantity	16mm	(.5")	$ 2.80	_____
_____	28mm	(.75")	$ 6.00	_____
_____	40mm	(1.5")	$13.00	_____
_____	50mm	(2")	$21.75	_____
_____	60mm	(2.75")	$35.00	_____

Sphere

	Size		Each	Total
_____quantity	20mm	(.75")	$ 9.00	_____
_____	30mm	(1.25")	$15.00	_____
_____	40mm	(1.75")	$27.50	_____
_____	50mm	(2")	$53.00	_____
_____	60mm	(2.5")	$85.00	_____

Mirrors

		Each	Total
_____quantity	4" octagonal	$ 5.00	_____

Shipping: ($5.00, orders over $50, please add 10%)   _____
Sales tax   (Florida residents only 6.5%)   _____

Total $ _____
($25.00 minimum please, prices good through 12/96)

Call toll free 1(800) Earth Design
Please see last page for Fax & Postal orders

Wind Chimes

(Standard chimes have mahogany shaped Octagon clapper, unless noted)

Qty..	Model#	Length	#Chimes	Price	Total
____	SP: Spiral	22"	15	$33.00	_____
	Gentle enchanting melody (Notes: A, B, C # no clapper)				
____	SPL: Spiral	26"	15	$44.00	_____
	Gentle enchanting melody (Notes: B, D, E, G #, A no clapper)				
____	Allegro	26"	16	$49.90	_____
	Staccato tone (Notes: G #, A, B, C #, D, E, F #, G #, A, B, D, E, F #, G #, A, B,)				
____	Celesta	22"	8	$35.00	_____
	Crystalline B minor 9th chord (Notes: B, C #, D, F #, B, D, F #, B)				
____	Minuet	18"	4	$18.70	_____
	Lilting 4 note harmony (Notes:A, B, C #, E)				
____	XS	20"	4	$22.00	_____
	Brilliant Harmony (Notes: G #, B, E,G #)				
____	XS8	24"	8	$30.80	_____
	East Indian scale (Notes: G #, A, B, D, E, F #, G # ,A)				
____	WCS	27"	8	$40.70	_____
	Shimmering harmony & overtones(Notes: G #, A, B, D, E, F #,G #, A)				
____	S8	31"	8	$46.90	_____
	Mystical Eastern scale (Notes: D, E, F #, G #, A, B, D, E)				
____	LC: Cathedral	72"	4	$83.00	_____
	Cathedral song (Notes: E, F #, G #, B)				
____	Finch	21"	6	$26.40	_____
	Pantothenic harmonics of the finch's song (Notes: E, F #, G #, B, C #, E)				
____	Lark	28"	6	$38.50	_____
	Pantothenic harmonies of a lark's flight song (Notes: E, F #,G #, B, C#, E)				
____	Dove	37"	6	$65.00	_____
	Low pitched dove-soothing song of peace (Notes: E, F #, G #, B, C #, E)				

Shipping: ($5.00, orders over $50, please add 10%)   _____

Sales tax   (Florida residents only 6.5%)   _____

Total ($25.00 minimum please) $_____

(prices good until 12/95, add 15% per additional year)

Call toll free 1(800) Earth Design
Please see last page for Fax & Postal orders

Earth Design
THE ADDED DIMENSION

Telephone orders: **Call toll free: 1 (800) Earth Design**
Please have your Visa/MasterCard ready.

Fax orders: (305) 751-9995

Postal orders: Earth Design, P.O. Box 530725,
Miami Shores, FL 33153

_____ copies **Earth Design**	$24.21	_____
_____ Natal birth chart	15.00	_____
_____ Local space chart	15.00	_____
_____ Natal & Local chart	25.00	_____

Shipping: book rate   _____
($3.00 for first, 75 cents each additional)

Sales tax   (Florida residents only 6.5%)   _____

Total $ _____

Please mail to: Name _____

Address_____

City/State/Zip_____

Birth information: Date_____Time_____Location_____

Local Space location:_____

Payment: ○ Check (enclosed)
○ Credit card: ○Visa ○MasterCard

Signature: _____
Print name on card: _____
Card number: _____Expiration: ___/___

Call _toll free_ and order now